ChaPTEr TwO -fOrmS Of ParENThOOd...................................... 37

Biological Parenthood 37
Foster Parenthood.............................. 40
Adoptive Parenthood......................... 42
Single Parenthood............................. 47
Teenage Parenthood........................... 52
Grandparents Raising Grandchildren................................. 54
Evolving Parenthoods.. 60

iii

Lesbian and Gay Parented Families................................ 60 Polyamorous Parenting................................ 63

ChaPTEr ThrEE: ParENTiNg aCrOSS diffErENT agES........................... 71

Infants (The First Year) 72
Toddlers (1-2 Years).. 74
Early Childhood (Preschoolers) (3-5 Years)........................ 76
Middle Childhood (6-8 Years)... 81
Late Childhood (9-11 Years)... 85
Early Adolescence (Teens) (12-14 Years)............................ 89
Middle Adolescence (15-18 Years).................................... 92
Late Adolescence (19-23 Years)....................................... 97

ChaPTEr fOur: ParENTiNg STylES aNd rOlE mOdElliNg................. 105

Authoritative Parenting (Just Right) 107
Authoritarian Parenting (Too Rigid)................................... 109
Permissive/Indulgent Parenting....................................... 110
Neglectful Parenting... 111
Qualities of a Positive Role Model.................................... 113
Balancing Work and Quality Time with Children..................... 118

ChaPTEr fivE: Child aBuSE.. 127

The Meaning of Child Abuse 128
State of Child Abuse in Kenya... 129
Forms of Abuse.. 131
Effects of Abuse... 137

Causes of Child Abuse...140

Interventions in Situations of Child Abuse and Neglect................140

ChaPTEr Six: diSCiPliNE aNd COrrECTiON fOr ChildrEN................ 145

Planning for Children's Discipline 147

Basics on Effective Discipline & Correction.............................149

Common Forms of Correction...150

Effective Versus Ineffective Correction.................................155

ChaPTEr SEvEN: dEaliNg wiTh COmmON BEhaviOr PrOBlEmS....... 159

Irresponsibility 159

Being Disrespectful..160

Teaching Your Child Good Manners.......................................161

Instilling Respect...163

Instilling Social Behavior...165

Instilling Honesty...166

Instilling Selflessness..168

Instilling Self-Control..169

Instilling Obedience...170

Management of Finances...170

Influence of Mass Media..171

Media Impact on Children's Behavioral Tendencies 174

Rules as a Strategy of Correcting Behavior.............................177

Parental Involvement in Children's Well-Being..........................178

Managing Sibling Rivalry...181

Parental Monitoring and Supervision....................................184

v

ChaPTEr EighT: ShaPiNg yOur Child'S malENESS aNd fEmalENESS.. 189

Gender is the First Form of Identity 189

Gender Stereotypes...192

Raising Boys...195

Parenting Teenage Boys...197

Raising a Boy as a Single Mother.......................................198

Advice on Parenting Boys...200

Raising Girls..205

Advice on Parenting Girls.. 206

rEfErENCES.. 212

PrEfaCE

This book seeks to provide an awakening for parents, challenging them to move away from stereotypical parenting styles to intentional, knowledge based parenting.

Parenting in the 21ˢᵗ Century calls for a different approach from parenting in the traditional African society. In the past, people were not as mobile as they are today and parenting was communal, with a lot of importance placed on children as the way of perpetuating society. The community felt duty bound to prepare children to ably take the mantle of procreation. Today's world is rapidly changing in light of education, careers and wealth creation. The family setup in general and parenting has indeed been affected by all these factors competing for attention. For instance, the ideal, traditional family setup (headed by one man, married to one woman) is no longer looked at as the ideal environment under which to raise healthy children. A growing number of women believe in the special donor concept where a woman gets a man solely to have a child and not a relationship/marriage with him, she then rears the child single handedly. This mindset does not look at the interests of the child and its impact on the child's growth.

This book aims at challenging parents to think about the "brands" of children they want. The book's clarion call is, *"What shall it profit you to advance in your career and make a lot of money but lose your child?"* Many find themselves thrust into parenting unprepared and thus become

candidates of challenged parenting. However, your child MUST not live the consequences of your ignorance, recklessness, lack of foresight, negligence and selfishness.

As a parent, teacher and therapist, I am all too familiar with challenges that today's children face. I have listened to diverse experiences from children and parents alike. Every child desiresan understanding, dedicated and knowledgeable parent, who responds appropriately to his or her needs.

In Kenya today, there are many cases of children becoming rebellious, reckless, truant, violent and some have availed themselves for radicalization, thus involving themselves in terrorism, sex trade and drug trafficking. This situation raises familiar but difficult questions, what went wrong so far as parenting is concerned? Are parents up to the task of guiding today's children or are there gaps that need to be addressed? Is it the parents' or children's fault?

When children are faced with any developmental and behavioral difficulties in any aspect of their life, the informed parent responds systematically, using measurable strategies. That is why every prospective parent should consider going through an effective parenting class before embarking on this awesome but important business of parenting. This would build in them capacity for quality and informed parenting and thus position them for any parenting challenges that may arise.

This book will be succeeded by *Effective Parenting Workbook* that will feature exercises and assessment tools. Facilitators of teams studying the workbook will have successfully undertaken a course on effective parenting and done a Trainer of Trainers course to qualify them to teach. The course will be conducted in schools, churches and in other religious facilities.

viii
ENdOrSEmENTS

Today, parenting seems like rocket science to many. This is because most parents are not keeping in step with the changes taking place, particularly technology-driven changes. Yet, God requires parents to guide their children well, *"Start children off on the way they should go, and even when they are old they will not turn from it"* (Proverbs 22:6). I highly recommend this book to churches, institutions, families, communities, counsellors and individuals.Those who invest in it are sure to find it a helpful guide in raising children.

rev. Edward Karanja K. (md)
moderator PCEa - Kiambu Presbytery

Catherine writes splendidly in thought provoking ways that puts recipients of the message on their toes yearning to change destinies for the better. Parenting is the cradle of responsible citizenship and the bedrock of a nation's mental health as she aptly puts it. This is 'a must' read for all counsellors, psychologists, other care givers and more importantly parents.

Kimani Githongo J.
Counselling Psychologist,
Chair, Kenya Counselling and Psychological Association (KCPA) &
Advocate of the High Court of Kenya

Catherine is candid that parenting in the 21st century requires training, coaching and retraining. The realities of the modern dynamic world have had great impact on families and more so parenting. Parents, guardians and caregivers require evidence based information to parent and nurture children adequately. This book provides well researched information that is handy for any parent and guardian in our times.

Prof. Philomena Ndambuki, Psychologist Kenyatta University
ChildrEN lEarN whaT ThEy livE
By Dorothy Law Nolte

If a child lives with criticism, he learns to condemn.
If a child lives with hostility, he learns to fight.
If a child lives with fear,
he learns to be apprehensive. If a child lives with pity, he learns to feel sorry for himself.
If a child lives with ridicule, he learns to be shy.
If a child lives with jealousy, he learns what envy is. If a child lives with shame, he learns to feel guilty. If a child lives with encouragement, he learns to be confident.
If a child lives with tolerance, he learns to be patient. If a child lives with praise,
he learns to be appreciative. If a child lives with acceptance, he learns to love.
If a child lives with approval, he learns to like himself. If a child lives with recognition,

he learns that it is good to have a goal. If a child lives with sharing,
he learns about generosity.

If a child lives with honesty and fairness, he learns what truth and justice are.
If a child lives with security,
he learns to have faith in himself and in those about him. If a child lives with
friendliness,
he learns that the world is a nice place in which to live. If you live with
serenity,
your child will live with peace of mind. **with what is your child living?**

Chapter 1

ChaPTEr ONE
BaSiC CONSidEraTiONS Of ParENTiNg

Having a baby is a life-changer. It gives you a whole other perspective on why you wake up every day
Taylor hanson

Parenting is The Bedrock Of a Nation's Sanity

Having your own child or children is an uplifting, invigorating and sacred experience. However, parenting is a scary obligation for most parents, riddled with lots of excitement, uncertainties and perplexing challenges. I once heard a guest in one of Kenya's national television stations remark that today's parent is bringing up 'broiler' children. She was comparing rearing today's child with rearing broiler chicken whose meat is tender unlike the tough but tasty indigenous birds.

She went on to explain that these children are ill equipped for the realities of the contemporary world. While outwardly they may have the deceptive look of people who are equipped, they are empty and obviously limited on the inside. They lack the agility, tenacity and resilience necessary to survive and succeed in the 21st Century. This is not unexpected in a world where parents value academic achievement, wealth accumulation and career progress over successful family life.

A healthy, progressive and dynamic nation is dependent on a workforce that is vibrant, resourceful, ethical and patriotic for its growth and posterity. The centrality of your role in contributing to nation building through rearing well-integrated children capable of adding value to their nation through equipping them with positive values, abilities and aptitudes cannot be over emphasized.Hence,parenting is the bedrock of a nation's sanity and development through production of accomplished children who eventually become dependable hardworking citizenry.

It is tragic for any nation to have unreliable, tactless and ill-informed parents who are not deliberate in developing a reliable work force and patriots for its nation. When children become vulnerable victims and inadequate adults, they become a liability to themselves, their families and the nation. We need to witness systematic government programs that aim to support purposeful parenting for realization of accomplished individuals. Your family legacy that spans through generations of resilient, robust individuals who form formidable marriages, families, entrepreneurs and career persons is reliant on your skilled, thoughtful parenting. Think long and hard and see that deep set inside you are deep longings for a life that is immensely valuable through responsible children. This implies you have to make a real investment in parenting your children purposefully to attain this deep satisfaction.

So even when parenting gets bumpy and demanding, do not quit, stay strong. Even when your parenting efforts do not seem rewarding, stay on course, you prayed to have children and its plentiful work to bring them up. You surely deserve your finish-line moment. The feeling at the end is sacred and benevolent, that smile that is deep set, those glistering eyes, that thankfulness, that sigh of relief as you look at your children surrounding your deathbed with a Godly satisfaction that you did your very best, you sacrificed for them, you trained them, you coached them, you mentored them, you disciplined them and you surrendered them to God. Gratefully, you permit yourself to close your eyes knowing you have run a perfect race. It is amazing and deeply spiritual to do this for your maker; you were simply a faithful custodian and in heaven, God says, *"Well done my good and faithful servant, enter into the Kingdom prepared for you"* (Matthew 25:21).

Effective Parenting requires Preparation

Children and youngsters sometimes develop high-risk destructive behaviors that are frightening for most parents. These can include, explosive temper tantrums, physical aggression, drug abuse and addiction, poor relating patterns, social media addiction, destructive or unhealthy sexual habits, fighting, planning and implementing school riots, suicidal ideations, committing suicide, promiscuity, threats or attempts to hurt others (including homicidal thoughts), teenage pregnancies, truancy, rebelliousness, habitual lying, disrespect for authority, refusing to obey rules and regulations, deliberately annoying people, blaming others for their own mistakes or misbehavior, getting easily annoyed, angered and spiteful, vindictive and intentional destruction of property among others.

Parents predispose their children to risky behavior orientation through parental neglect, ignorance, innocent irresponsibility and lack of selfdiscipline. As a parent, you have an obligation to provide deliberate and up-to-date parenting to your children so that they can grow into balanced, healthy individuals who will ably take on the world in a determined, well-versed manner. You have a crucial role of implanting protective mechanisms in your children so that they can stand unscathed by the difficulties and dilemmas of this life. Dr. Scott Peck, author of *The Road Less Travelled* starts his book with the statement "life is difficult"and indeed,it is.To help your child surmount a difficult world in a lifecycle, you need to inculcate relevant knowledge, tact and skillfulness in him/her. You definitely want them to be drivers of their own lives not passengers; when they are drivers, they are in control and they chart their own destination.

Effective parenting involves your preparation through training, willingness to be mentored by others, deliberately implementing parenting functions, taking feedback on parenting from your children and other close persons seriously and acting responsibly on it. Structural engineers and architects are careful to ensure that buildings they are in charge of have good foundations. Likewise, children require special attention during their formative years; since that is the time the foundation for healthy development is being formed. If, as a parent, you are not ready to learn so that you can practice responsible parenting, then you are not worthy being a parent. Moreover, every child requires the contribution of parents of both genders for him or her to experience wholesome growth mentally, relationally, spiritually, intellectually, emotionally and vocationally. Consequently, the best one can give his or her children is a functional marriage.

Most importantly, parenting children with a healthy worldview, selfdefinition, positive values and beliefs, capabilities and talents is like putting up a building that is meant to last long. You must be ready to fix in him or her 'columns' of abilities, capacities and healthy beliefs at particular focal points in the child's formative years. This foundation eventually becomes the holding base for future growth and resilience, and a launching pad for greater creativity and a wholesome life.

Many studies show that by age five to six, a child's personality is already concreted in him or her. Parenting is a demanding task and as a parent, you should be well equipped so that your rearing is well informed. Parents should develop a structured training program for each child, which should be evaluated and upgraded periodically. After all, parenting is just twenty-three years of focused; dedicated input and your child will be ready for takeoff. Proverbs 22:6 says, *"Train up a child in the way he should go, and when he is old, he will not depart from it."* This means, lessons learnt in early childhood are recalled and reused later in life. Moreover, parenting requires up-scaling and applying different approaches as children grow older and hence more independent. It is therefore sad that many approach parenting without first equipping themselves with the relevant skills to guide their parenting practices. Today, we are contending with a generation of children that seem overwhelmed by the demands of their world, so parenting needs serious rethinking if it is to effectively address the demands of the hour. Parenting creates different brands of children just like mechanical activities in factories produce different products.

So, what kind of children are you intending to rear? Do you have the relevant information to aid you to parent responsibly and adequately? What efforts are you making in order to have assured results? Evidence based parenting entails being assured that efforts you put in rearing your children will guarantee you 'outstanding children.' This is every parent's dream. You have to be sure that you can monitor and measure your parenting inputs; the care, protection, building abilities like cleaning, washing, polishing, compound cleaning, sustaining relationships etc.

Picture a child who has anger management problems. In the beginning of the year as you were taking stock of your children's needs, you and your spouse acknowledged that your second born child, Lincoln had anger tantrums that made him incapable of sustaining relationships or even nurturing them. He was even getting miserable with the rebuffs he was experiencing from friends. It was apparent he would have disastrous relationships in future if he was not coached to manage his anger problems, and that would in turn affect him as a worker and his perception of himself as a competent and worthy individual. In your yearly parenting plan for Lincoln, you have appreciated that he should be trained and coached on anger management and creating empowering relationships with others through the following:

a. Helping him to start listening to the emotion of anger inside him and identifying what causes it every time. He should be helped to closely monitor how that anger develops to the point he throws a tantrum. He might say, "My anger starts in my head by a thought I have, for example, the thought that I am not appreciated in this family. It then descends into my heart and I start having a rapid heartbeat, then I experience an adrenalin rush in my hands and I start sweating. At that time, I can slap someone, insult or even hit something." Monitoring the process of anger building gives the Lincoln the ability to disrupt this process so that anger can dissipate.

b. Get him to deal with anger appropriately for instance by talking to the person who has made him angry. He could say, "Mum, when you say I am good for nothing, I get the impression that you do not believe in me." This expression of his frustration helps him discharge the negative energy emanating from feeling put down.

c. If a situation is making him angry like not performing well, he can be helped to look at options that would steer him into attaining better performance instead of getting angry.

d. Helping him appreciate that 'anger is not bigger than him' and thus he should not allow it 'to manhandle him.' He can learn to talk to the anger or any other negative emotion by saying, "anger, you won't mess me up, I won't allow you to."

There are many parenting programs that are in existence today in counselling training institutes, churches or organizations whose key mission is empowering parents to be effective parents. As a parent, find out where such programs are offered and enroll. However, it is important to note that parenting is an experiential, dynamic, multifaceted responsibility, which has twists and turns, uniqueness, and emerging issues.

Even when you have attended training, there are times you feel lost, not knowing how to respond to your child's needs. That is normal and human; do not be distressed. This means you have to think through the new challenge and possibly consult others for you to be in a better position to respond adequately.

Though Wendy's mother attended a parenting course, it did not deal with all possible parenting concerns. You also may have realized that any parenting training that you may have attended does not give you 'microwave' solutions or it is never a 'one size fits all tactic.' Getting another parent or a counsellor to proactively discuss ways of dealing with the issue at hand would help. Besides, there is no school where you can graduate as a 'parent' after successfully completing a parenting course. You have to continually wade through the murky waters of parenting to learn how to be an effective parent. Wendy's mother is learning this the hard way. She understands well that anxiety and panic will not help her but somewhat looking at different ways that this issue can be tackled.

what Can we liken Parenting with?

Three analogies come to my mind that aptly capture the crux of parenting; baking a cake,farming and the thorough checkups performed on an airplane before takeoff.

Child rearing can be compared to the process of baking a delicious cake to celebrate people's successes and accomplishments. The chef starts by carefully measuring the ingredients so that they are in the right quantities before mixing them. The flour, eggs, margarine, sugar, baking powder, vinegar and other ingredients are first measured, then mixed and kneaded until they produce perfect dough. The task does not end there; when the cake is put in the oven to bake, the chef is always monitoring the condition of the oven to prevent burning or the cake being under cooked. Parents too have to always be on guard, providing the right ingredients (social, spiritual, emotional, physical, vocational and mental resources) for child nurture, necessary controls, guidance and provision if they are to produce healthy brands of children.

Child rearing can also be compared to a farmer who is growing a sensitive crop that demands very specific conditions. Such a farmer must be very careful how he approaches his work. After choosing the seed, the farmer is mindful about the right time to plant. He also ensures that the soil has the right nutrients for the seeds to germinate. Having done all that, he must make sure that he weeds periodically so that the weeds do not compete with the farmer's crop for the muchneeded nutrients. Parents too must have intentionality of what they plant in their children, ensure nurturance of those rudiments and be watchful of the competing threats so that they can be weeded out on time.

Child rearing can also be compared to the air traffic control system which provides assessment and travel advisories. The mandate of the engineers at the watchtower is to guide the flight safely, keep track of every phase of the flight movement and guide separation between the planes to avoid collisions or airplanes going missing. The taxiing of the airplane on the runway makes it gain momentum and enables the pilot ascertain it is ready for takeoff; even after it soars, there is no passenger movement until it gets into the aircraft flight path. Parents equally should ensure that the children they rear have a clean bill of fitness before they flag them off for takeoff to avoid tragedies.Takeoff for children means they are ready to contend with a real world and are able to engage the right gears for success. This means they are able to relate with themselves and others in healthy ways and their work ethics are above par.
In the three analogies above, relevant knowledge and experience are necessary for producing the right results. In the same way, investing in your children will be necessary to assure you of generations of outstanding individuals and families. Parenting is not a mean feat; it requires thorough preparation,reflective decisions and strict monitoring and evaluation that in turn inform the next parenting efforts. Parenting is not for the impatient who love quick fixes but for the very patient who understand that it is a lifelong pursuit.

what Parenting Entails

Parenting is the process of promoting and supporting the physical, emotional, social, spiritual, vocational and intellectual development of a child from infancy to adulthood. It refers to the activity of raising a child rather than the biological relationship. It has been impressed on me repeatedly as I counsel my clients that the informal education imparted by parents on their children has more impact on the children's lives than what is imparted by the formal education system. What a child gets through parental efforts and nurture become the background and beacons against which he/she functions. Hence, individuals can be highly educated but when it comes to skilled living, they score miserably. When you are parenting, you provide care, exposure, challenge, support, love and guidance to a child for healthy development.This means that you must create a nurturing environment that affords attention, experiment, encouragement and love for your child. Remember, what you do or do not do determines the kind of child your daughter or son becomes. Your child is a jewel, so your parenting should be well informed and systematically evaluated and monitored to ensure positive results.

Informed parenting may require spending regular time with support groups devoted to parenting or attending courses on effective parenting. As a parent, consider identifying a parenting consultant (therapist) to advise you on fundamentals of parenting for different stages in your child's development; there should be no shame in this.
I have counseled many children whose parents are caregivers like pastors,counselors/therapists,psychologists,human resource managers, communication experts, social workers and medical practitioners. These children express frustration and great disappointment that their parents are helpers and yet they fail dismally at parenting them adequately. I have come to appreciate the fact that no parent is beyond reproach when it comes to parenting. Hence, even caregivers should learn to consult parenting experts or peers for advice on how to raise their children.

As a mother of young adults and a therapist of more than fifteen years, I have learnt enough lessons to admit there are many times I am clueless when it comes to dealing with our children's difficulties and challenges. This admission is humbling and it makes me look up to my husband Gilbert so that we both can figure out what to do. We all have deficiencies in certain areas and therefore need others to guide us, direct us, evaluate us and help us take care of our grey areas in parenting. Moreover, you have to keep updating yourself with parenting knowledge, skills and capabilities to help you deal with the emerging needs of your child.

Some children are nurtured by other people and not their biological parents. These may be grandparents, older siblings, aunts, uncles, nonrelatives or professional care providers. As a parent, create healthy relationships with the extended family or 'secure caring others' so that your child can benefit from relating with them.

Pacy's Case
Mrs. Tumaini is a mother of one who feels she has completely failed in parenting. She is a Christian who serves diligently in church and has been looking up to the pastor in her church and the church elders to help her deal with her parenting challenge but reports they have not been there for her. She says Pacy, her only daughter, who currently is in form two, has turned out to be rebellious. She sneaks away from home at night and joins her male friends who have become her friends in her drinking sprees. To sustain this behavior, Pacy has been stealing from family members. As a result, they have come to detest her. Pacy says her mother does not like her and that the dad is not available for her.

Since her birth,Pacy's mother pampered her.When Pacy was three years,her grandmother expressed concern, warning Pacy's mother that Pacy would not amount to much with that kind of parenting but Pacy's mother adored her and would not let anyone discipline her. Over time, people noticed and started complaining that Pacy was growing up to be an insensitive girl who loved to receive but never give or listen to anyone's counsel. A nextdoor neighbor even warned that the mother would reap the fruits of her overprotective parenting when the girl became an adolescent.

The case of Pacy demonstrates gaps of knowledge and skills that Mrs. Tumaini had as she parented Pacy. She thought that by pampering her daughter and not instilling discipline in her, she was conveying love and protection. However, this backfired when Pacy turned out to be an insensitive, irresponsible individual who could not fit in a real world. No matter how difficult it is,Mrs.Tumaini has to allow Pacy go through pain and distress, to learn lessons she did not learn as a child.

are my Babies Safe with the maid (*Ayah*)?

It has become very scary to hire a caregiver because of the harrowing stories we hear all the time. Even as you may be scared to death, you cannot afford to be skeptical about the issue especially if you are a career person. Even when you are not, there are times you may need some help with your children. The 21th century presents different realisms about childcare that have to be addressed with caution. In the 20th century, families used to live in the same compound and getting a family member to help with rearing a child was the norm. Hence, children were brought up by family members who had a stake in their growing up.
Children too sense the insecurity when they are brought up by *ayahs* who are abusive and neglecting. They develop conflictual feelings regarding relationships and this gets ingrained in their personality development. A caring, loving ayah instills safety, stability and security in a child.

In a WhatsApp message that was circulated some months ago, a child asked his mother, "mum, would you leave your purse with money with our ayah?" The mother retorted, "Oh my, how can I do that my child, that's a crazy thing to do?" Smiling mischievously, the child voiced, "If you can't leave your purse with her, why do you leave me with her?"

This satirical story illustrates how careless we parents can be sometimes with our children while we are too careful with material things. The vignette illustrates the need for entrusting children to those we are certain they cannot hurt them. It also clarifies the essence of being sensitive to our children's needs. Have you taken stock of the emotional and survival needs an *ayah* should meet in your child? Please do, for your child entrusts you with this vital responsibility and expects you to pass the test of time.

Hiring a full-time help can be a big bonus as this will provide you the much-needed extra help as well as allow you some time off. Your house *ayah* is your 'back up' or 'supplementary' when you are not there to take care of your child; hence, you need to have your criteria of choosing a maid right. Nevertheless, before you hire an *ayah* (maid), either parttime or live-in, you need to consider a few things:

a. Where does she come from?

b. What reasons made her choose to be an *ayah*?
c. What is her level of education?
d. Is she trained as an *ayah* or are you ready to train her? e. What is her temperament like? Is she emotional with signs of

unresolved emotional issues?
f. Have you done a background check of where she comes from?

Her parents, her siblings and her morals
g. Have you connected with her family members and are you in agreement that she has to work for you?
h. Is she still a minor who requires personal development?
When children are brought up by other minors, they can be endangered by the minor's developmental inadequacies i. Is your live-in ayah going to care of the child only or will she
double up as a cook and housekeeper?
j. Have you given her a contract of her job role whether written or verbal? It is best to have a written contract
k. Have you told her about the dos and don'ts of your house? Is she comfortable with the regulations?
l. Have you identified her gaps that need to be filled? m. Do you have copies of her identification documents? E.g. ID,
photos

Once you have your mind set, start looking for someone who will fit the bill. Speak to family members, neighbors, friends and colleagues for recommendations, research and visit reputed maids' agencies. The *ayah* you choose should be mature (over 18 years old), decent, emotionally balanced, conversational, pleasant and respectful. If she has gaps in any of these key areas, you MUST be prepared to take her for some form of training, formal or informal. She too has to be willing to love your children, take care of them well and be playful with them.

Trained maids have a bearing of what to expect in their job role and know how to handle jobs efficiently. However, experience would help your *ayah* surmount the needs and challenges of rearing your young child. With training (by you or through a program), she will be able to cook, clean, look after the baby and handle a range of household chores. You may feel angry with a girl who is inexperienced or inadequate in some key roles, but remember we all require capacity building to be equipped in our job role. Take time to mentor and coach her to carry out her work adequately. Some *ayahs* maybe going through a delicate transition stage in their lives hence require your indulgence to understand and develop them. Picture a girl who is between 18 to 23 years, she has not fully developed and truly requires your input so that she can stabilize.

The Ugandan Ayah who Molested an Infant
In November, 22 2014, a shocking story of a Ugandan baby being tortured by a maid hit the headlines and social media. In a video clip, a two-yearold is seen terribly tortured by a maid, Jolly Tumuhirwe, 22. The toddler's father worked at a reputable NGO in Kampala and he was the one who released the video that was captured by interior security cameras and showed Tumuhiirwe trying to feed the baby. The baby, who was sick at the time, exhibited difficulty in coping with the rough and speedy rate at which Tumuhirwe fed her.

Tumuhiirwe then turned to the porridge and started eating it. But the toddler could not contain the stuffed food down her throat. She threw up dreadfully. This invited Tumuhirwe's wrath. She landed a hot slap on the kid before throwing her off the sofa, her face hitting the floor. She remained there for a few seconds before Tumuhiirwe followed her. Using a rechargeable torch, she clobbered her severely. She continued kicking her and stepping on her back.She finallygave her the last kick,which sent her silent and unable to move. Tumuhirwe then picked the baby like by one hand and vanished in the next room.

We do not know the reason Tumuhiirwe behaved the way she did. However, there is always a reason behind any behavior people exhibit. We were also given scanty details about the mother of this child and it would be interesting to know these missing details to complete the picture. How did the behavior of the maid get to this level with a mother who was said to be a house wife? An article in one newspaper indicated, "Efforts to get hints on the baby's mother were futile as family sources maintained silence on the question."

Your Relationship with your Child's 'Ayah'

Remember your children's caregiver requires respect and consideration from you and others in your home. She needs a collaborative and responsive relationship with you so that she can carry out her work sufficiently. You have to prepare those in your house to treat her in human ways even before she arrives. You are going to be leaving her with what you treasure most, your child, hence; she deserves utmost comfort and security for her to give the same to your children.

No one is allergic to love; she too will come out best when she is treasured by you. People thrive best in nurturing environments where their needs are met; she too. Notably, most of the girls we hire to take care of our children have gone through social and economic challenges for them to choose to work as *ayahs* while others come from conflict ridden families where they got inadequate care. You need to be cognizant of these factors even as you hire them because they affect their interpersonal relations with your household. Some reasons that make *ayahs* mistreat children in their care include:

a. Having emotional issues in their growing up that they have not resolved hence, they project them on children under their care
b. Feelings of rejection and unfairness from others thus becoming reactive to children they are rearing
c. When you mistreat them as an employer, they might turn their wrath on your children to punish you

You have to become a walk-mate, partner and a friend to your *ayah* in the journey of rearing your child. She has to sincerely feel she is growing and developing by rearing your child and working for you. Her experience in your house MUST be enhancing; this ensures the returns to you, and your child is worth the effort invested.

you are your Child's first Teacher

Many parents fear that they do not have what it takes to be effective parents. This is because some parents nowadays are inundated with responsibilities that leave them with little or no time for parenting. Others feel ill equipped for the full time job of parenting. In the present world, there are many things, particularly those associated with one's career, that are competing with parenting for attention. Yet many people want to excel in family life, in their careers and in other pursuits. It is unfortunate that effective parenting is not as celebrated today as it used to be in the Africa of the past.

As a parent, you have the responsibility of purposively teaching your children how to approach life and live out what you teach so that they can have a living example to fashion their behavior after. It is therefore important for you as a parent to be cautious of how you live your life. Moreover, you should intentionally plan for the lessons you want your children to learn. These may include desirable values, roles and responsibilities, self-care habits, effective ways of carrying out tasks, desirable behaviors and right attitudes. You should also go beyond instructing and barking orders to modeling the kind of behavior you intend to inculcate in them.

Dancy (2012) singles out the following as lessons you must teach your children:
a. Teaching your children how to wisely respond to different

situations.
b. Teaching and demonstrating healthy ways of expressing emotions.
c. Teaching your children personal hygiene, eating habits, relating in healthy ways and how to safeguard personal boundaries. d. Providing your children with exposure and opportunities to glean knowledge for their mental development.
e. Encouraging your children to express their ideas, ask questions and make responsible decisions.
f. Encouraging your children to make responsible choices and discussing their choices with them as they grow older. g. Allowing them to safely explore their environment so that they can learn to exercise healthy caution.

Effective parenting involves taking your responsibility seriously and taking advantage of every opportunity to enhance your children's learning by giving them tasks and supporting them to carry them out. Largely, children absorb life experiences indiscriminately and these life experiences influence their character, feelings and values, and provide the window through which they view the world. Accordingly, through interacting with your children, you can guide their growth and development. By age five, most children are exposed to school life, and you can provide them with learning experiences haphazardly or unknowingly (with good intentions, but with little knowledge and no plan) or you can consciously plan for quality experiences to occur and exercise your obligation in a more responsible manner.

Things Parents Can do To improve the learning Environment at home
Task 1: Learn More about How Children Learn

Parents who have been successful in their role as the first teachers of their children take time to appreciate how their children learn. The following are common facts regarding how children learn:

a. Children Are Always Ready to Learn
Children have an inborn capacity to learn. This innate willingness to learn can be nourished or weakened by childhood experiences from the environment. As a parent, you should:

• Turn as many everyday life experiences as possible into learning opportunities
• Model learning from everyday experiences
• Talk about the importance of learning as a self-initiated activity

b. Children Have a Curiosity for Learning
Children test the world with their curiosity to learn and understand.When a child jumps from a chair the first time and finds out that it hurts, he or she has learned the consequences of such an act. The responsibility of the parent is to teach the child that risks need to be calculated. Hence, as a parent you should:

• Take advantage of your children's questions to extend learning
• Capitalize on your children's interest in selecting learning experiences
• Plan the home environment with your children's needs and desires in mind
• Get playmaterials that are specificallydesigned to stimulate children's thinking and creativity

c. Children Learn from their Environment
Children learn from all aspects of the environment. The environment is represented by people and objects that surround them. Every experience, whether positive or negative, will teach children something. Hence as a

parent, you should:

• Expose your children to experiences that teach social, academic and motor skills
• Capitalize on your children's interest in selecting learning experiences
• Allow children to actively interact with the environment thus allowing them to explore and ask questions

d. Children Thrive in an Environment of Love and Respect Children need to feel secure in order to take risks and take advantage of learning experiences. Children who feel a sense of belonging and who feel valued explore their world with confidence. Hence, as a parent you should:

• Show love for all your children equally
• Celebrate the uniqueness of each child
• Respect your children's views of the world
• Provide opportunities for your children to excel and experience positive feelings about themselves
• Model respect for others' beliefs and values
• Teach your children to respect other people's beliefs and values

e. Children Have a Potential for Acquiring Language
Children learn from their parents and the persons with whom they live. Children have an innate capacity to process and use language. Talking and reading with children develops their learning of language. Once children have mastered one language, they can learn a second one quickly. Hence, as a parent, you should:

• Talk to children as often as possible
• Engage children in conversation
• Ask for their views about certain topics of interest
• Increase children's vocabulary on different topics

f. Children Can Communicate Ideas in Many Different Ways Children are versatile individuals who learn to communicate ideas through language, behavior and actions. Hence, as a parent, you should:

• Provide opportunities for your children to communicate ideas through

speech or writing
• Show children ways by which they can communicate ideas
• Encourage your children to use acceptable behavior
• Redirect unacceptable behavior
• Provide opportunities for your children to appreciate art and music

g. Children Can Acquire a Love and Desire for Reading

Reading is the most efficient way of acquiring information. Reading is a skill that children can develop from a very early age. As a parent, you should:

• Stress the importance of comprehending what is being read
• Provide opportunities for children to select topics or books to read
• Read to children at an early age
• Have print materials (newspapers, books, letters, regardless of their language) at home at all times
• Read labels and signs with children
• Expose children to different literature styles at an early age

h. Children Learn in Different Ways
Adults and children use the senses to learn. Parents should keep this information in mind and determine what the preferred ways of each child to learn are. As a parent, you should:

• Provide children opportunities to learn by using all the senses
• Teach children that some questions do not have a right or wrong answer
• Provide children opportunities for problem-solving using the different senses
• Provide children with opportunities to role play

Task 2: Establish a Vision and Goals

A vision is a mental picture of an event that has not yet occurred. A mental picture allows us to define what children would be able to do after a given period. Getting there does not, however, happen automatically; parents have to make sure that support is available to help children get to that point.

Hellen says to her five-year-old son, *"I know, Michael, you will grow up to*

*be a charming, hard-working boy who is mindful of other people. I am sure
you will work hard in school to the best of your ability and you will be
careful to do right. I can see you love learning many things and you take time
to understand what is new to you."* Michael looks at his mother and says,
"Mum, one day I will be the President." Hellen is already inculcating in
Michael the desire for hard work by making the boy aware that to be
outstanding, one needs to be disciplined and hardworking, and Michael
seems to pick it up in little ways. The lessons that follow should target on
instilling self-discipline, hard work, self-respect and respect for others. She is
giving Michael a world-view about himself and what would be useful to
focus on.

Task 3: Reflect and Plan an Enriched Learning Home Environment

The third major taskis to take stock,reflect and plan the home learning
environment. As a parent, you need a checklist of all items required to make
your home an enabling environment for your children.

adjusting to Parenting

The coming of every child requires you to take stock of what the child will
need physically, emotionally, relationally, educationally, financially and
spiritually to grow healthy. Parents who are conscious of the challenges
awaiting them prepare for the coming child. It is important for you to know
that the coming of a child in your family is going to impact on your time,
space, material resources and emotional resources. You should therefore
reorganize yourselves in terms of your expectations, rules, roles, behavioral
patterns, budgeting and general interactions.

Rehema's Case
*Rehema was excited to get another child after ten years and assumed that she
would automatically cope. She had looked forward to getting a baby boy and
here it was. However, after delivery, she started feeling low and out of place.
She thought she was fatigued from the delivery, but the experience persisted.
She had not counted the cost of re-learning how to take care of a young one.
She was particularly getting irritated by the child crying at night and making
her stay awake throughout the night. She did not get better until she visited
her therapist who told her she had not taken a realistic stock of the emotional*

energy a child required from a mother when small. The therapist helped her create a wider emotional container for the child so that she could accept what she could not change rather than wrestle with it. When she did that, she developed inner peace and allowed herself to rest when she could.

Having a child introduces a major lifestyle realignment that can be very stressful. The case of Rehema brings home the reality that parenting is a full time job that must not be approached with unpreparedness and assumptions. She thought she could handle the coming of another child with ease but she later realized that emotionally she had not created enough space for the new one. Accommodating a child means that you have defined how different life will be when the baby arrives and ways in which you will need to extend yourself. When you do, even the newborn's cries and shrieks will not destabilize you and you will be able to take them within your stride.

Certain circumstances call upon you to adjust so that you can parent effectively. These include single parenting, change of work, separations, divorce, life transitions, chronic sickness of a family member, having a child with disabilities,or/and having limited finances.Children,too,are affected by the circumstances under which they live. A study by Amato (2005) reports that young children who live with people other than biological parents or those from single-parent households are less likely to exhibit behavioral self-control than children living with two biological parents. This means that children have less inner conflicts and emotional problems when they are brought up by their biological parents. When this is not the case, they grapple with questions regarding their ancestry, which leaves them lost and dejected. Amato further argues that children living with two married adults (biological or adoptive parents) have, in general, better health, greater access to health care, and fewer emotional or behavioral problems than children living in other types of families do.

According to Amato, outcomes for children in step-parent families are, in many cases, similar to those for children growing up in singleparent families while children whose parents are divorced also have lower academic performance, social achievement, and psychological adjustment than children with married parents. This confirms that divorce traumatizes children thus interfering with their vital abilities. For you as a parent, you are most probably very distressed and therefore incapable of providing your children the emotional support required to deal with accumulated losses they suffer (loss of relationships, normalcy and finances among others). Reliance on kin networks (for example living with grandparents) can provide social and financial support for some families, particularly single-parent families.

Single-parent families tend to have much lower incomes than do twoparent families, whereas cohabiting families fall in between. Amato's study indicates, however, that the income differential only partially accounts for the negative effects on many areas of child and youth wellbeing (including health, educational attainment, behavior, and psyche) associated with living outside of a married, two-parent family. Evidence from this study can help you make informed decisions regarding your parenting. For instance, as a single parent you can decide to create healthier relationships with your larger family so that your child can have more relationships that can influence his or her life positively.You mayeven want to find ways of expanding your income base so that you can provide the financial needs of your child easily.

For parents who do not live together, it is important to cooperate with each other for the benefit of the children. In my experience as a therapist,I have confirmed repeatedly that children adjust more easily to crisis and loss if their parents work together to develop healthy ways of communicating,resolving problems,and reducing conflict.Manning and Lamb (2003) affirm that children brought up in a single parent family require responsible honesty from their parents. Such parents need to ensure their children get consistent mentorship, whether professionally or informally provided by a caring person. It is important for you to remember that the formation of a positive parent-child relationship is a life-long process.

Moreover, the key to a successful parent-child relationship is the quality of time, not the quantity of time spent together. Whether you are a single parent, divorced and parenting, adoptive parent, foster parent or even two biological parents, what informs effective parenting is identification of inherent needs manifest in each situation and respond to them with thoughtfulness, understanding and proactivity.

As a parent:
a. Understand the particular challenge you have.

b. Accept the particular situation you are going through, if it

cannot be changed.
c. Identify ways of handling the challenge so that it does
not interfere with effective parenting, and adjust through
identifying suitable strategies.
d. Attend training or coaching sessions on challenges such as the
one you are going through.
e. Get a mentor of the same sex with the child you are parenting
single-handedly if he or she is not of your gender. f. Receive therapy together
with your child if professional help is
deemed necessary.

Qualities of an Effective Parent

a. adaptability
This is the ability to change your practices to suit emerging issues in
parenting and improve your parenting skills. This shows you are flexible and
easily notices options you can choose from in responding to your child's
needs and personality.

b. Sense of humor
This is the ability to take things easy, despite the challenges of parenting. It is
an indication that you can afford light moments and you are able to cope
easily with the frustrations of life.

c. mature
This is a state of having grown beyond the childhood experiences to achieve
personal stability. When as a person, you are psychologically stable, you are
able to support your children by giving them love, care and guidance.

d. Positive attitude toward Self
This involves self-appreciation, being aware of and comfortable with the self.
When you accept your strengths and weaknesses, you are in a position to
accept your children as they are and promote their self-esteem.

e. Emotionally Secure
Parents who do not feel threatened emotionally and therefore do not depend

on others for a sense of value allow their children to be who they are.
Accordingly, you are able to handle both positive and negative feedback.

f. Patient
Children require a lot of patience as they experiment and explore their
environment. When you are a patient parent, you are able to accommodate
your children's individual differences. You are also able to "come down" to
the level of your children.

g. Sense of integrity
Parents who are honest and have good morals qualify as positive role models
for their children. When you have earned your children's respect,you are able
to influence them.

h. Team effort
Parents who work together show a strong sense of purpose to their children.
Such parents inculcate in their children a sense of collective responsibility in
managing family affairs, thus preparing them for adult responsibility.
Through team effort, children's varying needs are adequately met.

undesirable Parenting Practices
The following are practices considered harmful in parenting because they
have negative effects on children.

a. unrealistic Expectations
Parents with unrealistic expectations demand too much or too little from their
children. Expecting too much from your children overstretches their abilities.
In many cases, this causes intense frustration and leads to giving up. If, on the
other hand, you expect too little from your children, you fail to provide them
with the necessary challenges to grow. As a result, you kill their creativity,
thus making them feel bored, inadequate and dependent. Both over expecting
and under expecting limit children's rate and level of maturity.

b. indulgence
This is where you anticipate your child's needs and try to meet them even
before the child is aware of them or even before the child calls for help. Such
parental behavior creates dependence in the children, thus affecting their
ability to take responsibility of their lives and have self-direction.

c. Submissiveness

This is the situation where you give in to all your children's demands (desires and wishes) even when they are unrealistic. You therefore do not model appropriate rights, limits and boundaries to your children. Such children grow without selfcontrol and regard for others' rights.

d. Overprotection

Overprotective parents cushion their children from life's challenges, blocking them from trying new tasks; hence, such children fail to develop courage and become independent.

e. Belittling

Children have their own rights that need to be respected. When you belittle your children, they in turn degrade themselves and fail to develop positive self-concept with adequate self-esteem and healthy identity.

f. Neglect

Neglecting parents fail to give their children adequate time for nurturance. As a parent, you ignore your children's needs for providence, attention and encouragement. Children may lack the ability to form close and meaningful relationships in future due to fear of rejection. From within, they experience a sense of rejection and they normally reject others before they are rejected and therefore cannot withstand temporary strains in relationships.

g. rejection

Rejecting parents are unwilling to accept responsibility for care and development of the child. They exclude children in their lives and ignore their needs. For you to do this you may have been rejected yourself and therefore you are physically mature but emotionally immature. Children grow up confused, lonely and feeling abandoned and may never know how to love and take care of other people.

Segei's Case
Segei, 19, had a mixture of admiration and resentment for his father, Mandi, who was a drunkard and thus wasted all his monies through this irresponsible lifestyle. When drunk, he would insult his son, dismissing him as useless and a poor performer in school. In his drunken stupor, he lamented audibly that he did not expect his son to amount to anything. As a

result, Segei felt rejected, neglected and worthless; twice, he attempted suicide. To deal with his guilt and make up for his mistakes, Mandi, when sober, would buy his son all sorts of things.

Segei's mother could notice that her husband's attitude towards their son left much to be desired, hence she complained but also urged him to attend parenting training or counselling sessions but he could not hear any of that. On the flip side, Mandi was submissive, quiet and withdrawn when sober. Mandi's wife was perpetually worried about their son Segei, who she felt, lacked a mentor in the father. Inside her, she could hear the shrill voice of her spiritual director saying, "Parenting is not for cowards."

Segei would have wanted to be loved and celebrated by his father but this never happened. Though Mandi's wife cajoled him to seek assistance or training in parenting, he flatly refused; a widespread scenario in many households. What Mandi did not realize is that he was sabotaging himself bydestroying his son through deficient,uninformed parenting. The result was that Segei became an incompetent insecure child who did not develop self-love and positive regard.

roles and responsibilities of Parenting

Responsible parenting entails knowing what you want your child to be in future and working towards achieving it.The parental responsibilities listed below shape a child's physical, mental, spiritual and emotional well-being

Parental Responsibility Specifics

Provide an
environment that is safe

Provide your child with basic needs
Provide your child with self-esteem needs
Teach your child morals and values

- Keep your child free from physical, sexual and emotional abuse
- Keep unsafe objects locked up or out of reach of your child
- Get to know your child's caregivers (get references or conduct background checks)
- Take care of any potential dangers around the house
- Take safety precautions: Use smoke and carbon monoxide detectors, lock doors at night, always wear seatbelts when driving, etc.

- Water

- Plenty of nutritious foods
- Shelter
- A warm bed
- Medical care as needed/medicine when ill - Clothing that is appropriate for the weather

conditions
- Space (a place where he or she can go to
be alone)

- Accept your child's uniqueness and respect his or her individuality
- Encourage (don't push) your child to participate in a club, activity, or sport
- Notice and acknowledge your child's achievements and pro-social behavior
- Encourage proper hygiene (to look good is to feel good)
- Set expectations for your child that are realistic and age-appropriate
- Use your child's misbehavior as a time to teach, not to criticize or ridicule
Develop mutual
respect with your child

- Honesty
- Respect
- Responsibility - Compassion - Patience
- Forgiveness - Generosity

Provide discipline which is effective and appropriate

Involve yourself in your child's education
Get to know your child

Inculcating a sense of responsibility and work culture
Provide your child with spiritual grounding

- Use respectful language
- Respect his or her feelings
- Respect his or her opinions
- Respect his or her privacy
- Respect his or her individuality

- Well thought out
- Effective strategies
- Structured
- Consistent
- Predictable
- Fair

- Communicate regularly with your child's teacher(s)
- Make sure your child is completing his or her homework each night
- Assist your child with his or her homework, but do not do the homework
- Talk to your child often about school (what is being studied, any interesting events, etc.)
- Recognize and acknowledge your child's academic achievements

- Spend quality time together
- Do not take your child to boarding school when he/she is in class six and below; the school

environment does not adequately provide your child all-round nurture
■ Know your child's friends so that you can encourage beneficial relationships
■ Be approachable to your child
■ Ask questions and listen to understand
■ Communicate…communicate…
communicate

■ Give your children leadership and
managerial roles and supervise the outcomes

■ Helping the children take charge of tasks and attain excellence in carrying them out
■ Review with your child how the tasks were carried out and what should be improved
■ Reward attainment of responsibility and accomplishment of tasks
■ Reward innovativeness and volunteerism

Promote your child's manliness and
womanliness
■ Teach your child the importance of prayer

and how to pray
■ Children need to know that when their
human power and strength comes to an end,
they ought to trust in God
■ Let your children appreciate that spirituality
provides them with meaning and purpose for
life in all situations
■ Identify some nourishing spiritual programs
that your child should attend

■ Celebrate your child's gender through affirmation. For instance, you can tell your girl child, "You are
a pretty responsible girl who has abilities to take care of herself and

others." ■ Give your children opportunity to affirm and
celebrate their maleness or femaleness■ Teach facts about being male and female■ Buy books that
teach them about being male or female

responsibilities you do NOT have as a Parent
The following is a list of responsibilities that you are not expected to meet as
a parent:
a. Supplying your child with the most expensive designer clothes

or shoes available
b. Picking up after your child or cleaning your child's room when
he or she is of age
c. Dropping everything you are doing to give your child a ride
somewhere
d. Providing your child with a cell phone, television, computer,

ipad or game system
e. Bailing your child out of trouble every time he or she does
something wrong
f. Maintaining an unlimited supply of treats, chips, sodas, or junk
foods for your child
g. Replacing items your child has lost or misplaced
h. Welcoming all your child's friends into your home for social or
other activities
Forms of Parenthood

Chapter 2

ChaPTEr TwO
fOrmS Of ParENThOOd

Studies show that children best flourish when one mom and one dad are there to raise them.
John Boehner

There are different forms of parenthood, each with its own challenges, advantages and threats. However, there are some forms of parenthood that are more threatened and complicated than others. With any form of parenthood, however, forming a secure attachment with your child, which is the base of parenting, takes years of intentional parenting to develop. Common forms of parenthood include biological parents, foster parents, single parents, adoptive parents, step-parents, divorced parents and cohabiting parents.The familyis,however being redefined, as a result of which there are other parenting arrangements.As a parent, you need to appreciate the dynamics of your form of parenthood so that you can deal with them successfully. You have to contend with the challenges and threats posed by your form of parenthood. Once you have quantified them, it becomes easy to figure out how to overcome them for the good of your children.

Biological Parenthood

A study by Parke (2003) showed that children raised by their biological parents in a stable household usually have more advantages than children raised by foster parents, adoptive parents, step-parents, divorced parents, cohabiting parents, or in other parental arrangements. People are able to deal with challenges that emanate from natural arrangements as opposed to alternative arrangements.In my experience as a therapist, it has occurred to me that children reared by biological parents have lower levels of emotional difficulties when they have conflicts with their parents as compared to children not brought up by biological parents. It is usual to hear a child brought up by a nonbiological parent say, "I know they are treating me like this because I am not their child." However, having two parents is not enough; it is the practical presence of two *biological* handy parents that seems to support a child's development. In other words, children do not just need any two parents; they need parents who keep tab with their life's experiences and are responsive to their developmental needs.

Another study by Moore, Jekielek, and Emig (2002) establishes that the family structure matters for children, especially a family headed by two biological parents in a low-conflict marriage. Compared to children who are raised by married parents, children in other family types are more likely to achieve lower levels of education, to become teen parents, and experience physical health, behavioral, and mental health problems. This assertion rings very true when I relate it to my counselling experience with different forms of parenthood but also note that maladaptive marriages have equally negative impact on children brought up by both biological parents.

Prior to becoming a therapist, I was a high school teacher and I contended with children's anguish as they decried their parents' worsening marriage situations. It was evident that their parents' underachieving marriages profoundly affected their emotional and social states and had negative impact on their academic performance.

A broad study carried out among 20,000 children by McLanahan, and Gary (2009) in the United States of America revealed that children who grow up in a household with only one biological parent are worse off, on average, than children who grow up in a household with both of their biological parents. Poll results indicated that it is the child's relationship to their biological parents that matters, not just having two parents. This study can help you appreciate that both you and your spouse have to endeavor to create an enabling relationship with your children to facilitate their ability to be open to their own experiences and to critically evaluate different situations of life based on possible aftermaths and results.

Edith's Case
Edith was the first-born child of a single parent and was brought up in her grandparents' household. When she was in high school, her mother developed a chronic illness and died before Edith completed form four. Her aunt, a sister to her mother, who was almost her age, used to taunt her, telling her that she did not belong to that household. This made Edith have low self-worth and to always regard herself as unimportant. She feared attempting anything, even what she deemed she could manage. In response to her aunt's insensitive remarks, she generally worked unduly hard to prove herself. In a counseling session one day, she decided to talk about her dad

whom she had never talked about or grieved for. She talked about how she longed to know her father and how that would make her feel whole as a person. She remarked that if her dad were there for her as she grew up, she would not have contended with the challenges that made her have intense internal conflicts.

Edith's story helps us appreciate that children flourish best when both parents are present to rear them. Children brought up by guardians have deep-seated questions regarding their parentage. There is an inherent longing in every child to want to know both their parents; and there is tranquility and assurance that comes with knowing that both parents are committed to guaranteeing their welfare. They are readily able to accept themselves and be proactive in developing themselves.

foster Parenthood

A foster parent is a person who acts as parent and guardian for a child in place of the child's natural parents but without legally adopting the child. You may have done that occasionally and you may be doing it now. Foster parenting can be a thrilling experience when you do it through choice, this means you are not under coercion. Children benefit a lot when an adult steps in to play the role of a parent. Children are placed in foster care for different reasons. Sometimes their families cannot provide them with basic safety and protection. Many have also faced difficult experiences, including substance abuse by parents, sexual or physical abuse, relocation, displacement or abandonment. This might put a child in a situation where he/she is separated from the biological parents.

Foster parenting is the best option given the crisis that a family maybe exposed to. In Kenya, many adults choose to provide foster parentage to children so that they can provide them with loving care, coexistence, schooling and sustenance.

When a child is going through a difficult time or a transition, you provide continuity for the child when the parents are not able to provide parenting. By becoming a foster parent, you can give a child a chance to heal or feel sheltered during this difficult time in their lives. Foster parenting is not easybecause you have to find an emotional connection with the child through developing an empowering relationship with him/her. You should help the child perceive you as an approachable, friendly person. This way, the child will talk to you about any emotional challenges he/she maybe going through as he/she adjusts and deals with issues that have made him/her need a guardian. The connections you make with a child through foster care and the good role modeling you offer them can have a lifetime benefit for the child.

Claudia's Case
Claudia started staying with a foster parent when her mother died. She was in form two in a national high school and she did not know how to pick up from there. Her hopes of ever becoming an 'important' person that her mother had dreamt of were ruined. Other relatives did not want to take her to their homes. She was a liability to them. However, Janet, a single mother looked at her as she sang in the church choir one day and decided she would educate and take care of her. Claudia immediately struck a very close relationship with Janet's children and since she was older, she became their mentor. Janet realized she had grown to love Claudia as her own child.Claudia finished high school and was admitted to the University of Nairobi to study law. Two years ago, she completed law school and is now employed by an international organization. Claudia loves Janet who has become like a mother to her. She fondly calls her 'mum' Janet. Claudia's relatives now want her to stay with them but she does not have an emotional bond with them; she says they abandoned her when she needed them most.

Benefits of Foster Parenting

Emotional Benefits
It feels good to know you have made a difference in a child's life. Foster children can bring joy and happiness to you. Knowing that you have provided a warm, loving, and caring environment for a child gives you deep satisfaction.

Social Benefits

You have an opportunity of contributing to improving a child's life so that he/she too learn the importance of improving other people's lives. It provides you with an opportunity to give back to the community. If you have your own children, their lives get enriched through interacting closely with children whose backgrounds differ from their own.

Foster Parenting calls for the Following:

a. Providing for the child or children in your care
b. Creating emotional space within yourself and a physical one in your home
to contain the child so that he or she does not
become a burden to you
c. Always keeping the parents of the foster child updated on the
progress of their children
d. Facilitating the child's bonding with your family members e. Taking up the
responsibility of dealing with the emerging needs
of the child (medical care, emotional care, spiritual care, etc.) f. Devising an
effective way of disciplining the child who is
sensitive to punishment

adoptive Parenthood

An adoptive parent is a person who takes a child of other parents as his/ her
own through legal means. If you satisfy all the legal requirements of adopting
a child who is not your biological son or daughter, you have the right to
parent him or her. Any single or married adult whom the court determines to
be a "fit parent" may adopt a child. When you become an adoptive parent,
you are responsible for the child in all ways – legally, financially,
emotionally, spiritually, and relationally, just as if the child is your biological
offspring.

Getting to adopt a child in Kenya is a painstaking process that takes months
or years to be completed. This is simply prohibitive and many 'would- be'
parents shy away from initiating the process. Kenya lacks a comprehensive
policy for effective regulation and management of child adoption. In Kenya,
many children in the streets and in orphanages can benefit from having
adoptive parents.

Charlsie's Case
Charlsie is a form three student at Bright Hill Academy. She is from the Rift
Valley region and has been suspended from school because of being truant.
She is a quiet, withdrawn girl who has a lot of hatred for her adoptive

parents, both working. Her performance in primary school was dismal and her parents are worried this trend is continuing in high school. Charlsie has no friends, does not like to do anything and always feigns sickness so that she can be excused from school. Her parents adopted her when she was two years old,after finding her abandoned by the roadside. She wore bedraggled clothes and close inspection of her body revealed that she had been raped.

Her sorry condition notwithstanding, she was a beautiful child and the family agreed to adopt her. Today, her parents are worried because of her outbursts of anger, poor performance in school, keeping to herself all the time and open outrage at them. Although they accept her as their child and therefore have an obligation to take care of all her needs, they do not know how to help her live a happy, contented and successful life.

The case of Charlsie is sobering and leaves many questions unanswered. What would make Charlsie act the way she does? Why all the hatred, resentment and not wanting to do anything? Where is her energy and concentration? Had she been told she was an adopted child? How was it communicated to her? Was she allowed to grieve and let go of her biological parents? We cannot assume Charlsie should have been grateful for getting loving adoptive parents. There are issues disturbing her and they should be addressed particularly with a counsellor or psychologist. Children feel respected when they are given facts about their lives and this helps them concentrate on other aspects of life.

Common Reasons for Adopting a Child

The following are some of the most common reasons for individuals and couples to adopt a child:
a. Inability to get a child of your own due to infertility
b. Having a medical condition that hinders you from carrying a pregnancy to term
c. Being single, yet wanting to be a parent
d. Having a compassionate heart and wanting to use adoption as the way to start or expand your family
e. Simply using adoption as your option of having a child

Adoption can add to the trauma that a child has experienced, and trauma changes the brain chemistry. Often, there are traumatic events that will have led to the need for adoption, and this can negatively influence a child's abilities and behavior. The specific behaviors and disorders that occur because of trauma should be established so that a child is provided with the tools to facilitate healing and moving on with life.

Typically, adopted children are taken from the environment they have known and placed in a brand new one with people they do not know well. They must therefore be supported to grieve and let go so that they can sufficiently bond with members of the new family. The adoptive family should not expect the child to immediately start enjoying their new situation or be willing and capable of following the rules and culture of the new family.

An adopted child may come from a different background, street, residential house or culture. Hence, such a child should be treated with understanding and patiently given time to adjust to the new family. Adoptive families must be on the lookout for any signs of attachment strain and therefore do everything they can to promote efforts to fit in.

An Adopted Child Has Special Needs

Many adoptive parents in Kenya have not come to appreciate that unlike the child who has grown under his or her biological parents, an adopted child like Charlsie has special needs that require informed methods to deal with. Being removed from one's natural parents and surroundings disorients a child and interferes with his/her identity formation. People naturally crave the familiar, their ancestral roots. This provides them with a sense of belonging. Verrier (1993) argues that doctors and psychologists now understand that bonding does not begin at birth; it is a continuum of physiological and spiritual events which begin in the uterus and continues throughout the post-natal period. When this natural evolution is interrupted by a post-natal separation from the biological mother, the resulting experience of abandonment and loss is indelibly imprinted in the subconscious mind of the child, causing what is called the primal wound.

Verrier further offers that every adopted child at some point in his or her development has been deprived of this primitive, yet natural, relationship with his mother. Adopted children go through periods of adjustment and developmental challenges as they grow. Besides the common developmental issues, an adopted child, unlike one growing under the care of biological parents,finds himself or herself contending with other unique issues and concerns. These are brought about by a sense of being different, experiencing deep-set trauma, sense of loss, being assailed by grief, anxiety, panic, abandonment, lack of identity, rejection, depression, attachment difficulties and low self-esteem.

The feeling of loss and grief is common among many adopted children, and it results from not being raised by biological parent(s). Adopted children, especially those adopted late in life or adopted from foster care, may also find themselves dealing with the loss of siblings, grandparents, and other significant people who were, or might have been, part of their life. The development of identity is important throughout childhood but typically becomes more focused during adolescence. Unresolved issues can manifest themselves during that time in dramatic and destructive ways that adoptive parents may not be prepared for.

Adoptees Require Intensive Counselling

Identity development can be more complicated for an adopted child since questions keep coming up about why they were placed for adoption in the first place, who their biological parents were or are, where they are, what these biological parents do, how they look like, why they rejected him or her and a host of other questions which keep haunting them. The adolescent may also focus on the question of whom they really are and where they really belong. These are very difficult questions, and sometimes the adoptive parents may fear addressing them, lest they hurt the child. Hence, the adopted child and the adoptive parents need help to deal with questions about the adoptee not growing up with their biological parents and help resolve the attendant feelings of loss and lack of identity.

Sheila's Case
Sheila, 14 years old, feels different and alienated in her adoptive home. She is the last-born in a family of three children, the other two being biological children of her parents. One day she whispered to her teacher, "My worst moment is when my siblings are telling their life histories. Their eyes glow and they are excited about their ancestry, but I have nothing to say myself.

What do I tell when my life is shrouded in secrecy? My siblings can see themselves in the mirror of life, but I have nothing to see except blankness that fades into oblivion. Many times I feel lonely and disconnected as if I am floating in two worlds like a ghost.Who can help me?"

Sheila feels empty and lost; she considers herself different in very negative ways. She would love to know more about herself but this information is not availed; maybe because significant others do not know how much they can tell and what would be the impact; or they do not have essential information regarding Sheila. She says she needs help to fill in the gaps she experiences.

Needing outside help is common, and many adoptive families should seek post-adoption assistance for themselves and the adopted child. Counselling is needed to facilitate the child deal with issues that brought about adoption and promote sufficient bonding so that all the parties can work together towards greater assimilation and personal growth.From the time a child is adopted,contact with an expert adoptive counselor should be made to help in the development of healthy bonding with the adoptive family and identify any developmental issues and ways of resolving them.

There should be a ceremony to absorb her or him into the family and which should mark entry into the family. Adoptive children should be told the truth in special, loving ways so that they can deal with emerging issues with finality. If a child asks, "What made my parents abandon me?" The adoptive parents may say, "We may not be able to tell clearly what was happening to your parents at that time, but we are ready to be your parents and to take care of you as long as we live." The adoptive parent should avoid saying negative things about the child's parents.

Adoption can be the sweetest decision an adult can make, or the most harrowing experience of his or her life if the right steps of parenting an adoptive child are not taken.

Single Parenthood

McLanahan and Gary (2009) posit that being raised in a single-parent home poses significant risks to an adolescents'physical and emotional health; hence, ways of countering these risks should be formulated so that such children too can grow to be healthy. Children growing up in single-parent families, children born to unmarried mothers, and children in step-families or cohabiting relationships face higher risks of poor outcomes than do children growing in families headed by two biological parents. McLanahan, and Gary clarify that single parenthood, also called lone parenting or solo parenting, is the form of parenting where one adult cares for one or more children without the assistance of another parent in the home.

Single parenthood has always existed in all societies and should therefore not be viewed as deviant or problematic rather as an alternative form of parenthood. Stories of bravery regarding victories and challenges in single parenthood should be told more often so that best practices can be shared and employed for best results. Regardless of howthe change in familydefinition is viewed,the increase in families headed by one parent has a major influence on the social, economic and structural context of family life.

Matendo's Case
Matendo used to perform very well in school and was always lauded by his family for excellent performance. He was brought up by his mother single–handedly.She never married after she got her first child.Matendo used to ask where his father was when he was in primary school but his mother was tight-lipped on this issue.

When he sat for the national examination, he passed very well and was admitted to a highly regarded secondary school. When Matendo was in form three, the mother revealed his father's identity. As it turned out, the father had gone through the same high school and Matendo started looking for information about his father from the school records. What he found out made him change drastically from then on. He stopped taking his studies seriously and failed to take care of his personal hygiene and as a result, he became the laughing stock of other boys but he did not seem to mind this. Accordingly, he did not perform as well as expected in his O-level exams. From here, he was admitted to a public university and even given a scholarship but only attended a few lessons and dropped out of the university. However, that was not the end of his life's downward spiral. He gave up on his life's goals and found comfort in marijuana and other hard drugs. As a result, his mother was devastated but did not know what to make of this change in behavior.

A closer look into the life of Matendo shows that when the mother revealed the information the boy had been looking for, she did not provide him with an opportunity to process the information adequately. As a result, the wrong perceptions her son developed about his father resulted in depression, a condition that was never diagnosed because his issue was not handled by a counseling psychologist. It is important for parents to take care how they divulge information about the other parent because it can traumatize the child and incapacitate him/her for life.

Circumstances leading to Single Parenthood

Circumstances that lead to single parenthood are varied and each one of them presents unique variables and challenges that need to be clearly understood for the child to be supported effectively. These include extramarital pregnancy, separation, divorce, widow/widowerhood, adoption, artificial insemination, surrogate motherhood, single parenthood by choice and abandonment by the other parent

Strengths of Single Parenthood

a. Children in single parent families tend to become competent, helpful, independent and responsible faster than other kids.
b. Such children learn how to deal with adversity and change, particularly if they have lived through the divorce of their parents or the stigma of being in a home where there has always been just one parent.
c. Where there had been ongoing conflict between the parents, a change to living with only one parent could have positive effects on the children, such as gradual lessening of anxiety. It is better for children to see no relationship modeled to them rather than have a poor model when parents are living together in a highly conflictual relationship.
d. If the single parent is consistent in discipline and tries to be objective in all aspects of parenthood, the child can grow up to be healthy

Challenges of Single Parenthood

a. Sometimes as a single parent, you can feel like you are all alone, struggling

along the path of life without any external help.
b. You may find it difficult to have sufficient time with your children, and especially if you work away from home; therefore, your children may end up spending a lot of time alone.
c. If you were married before, it is normal for transition to single parenthood to be fraught with challenges, and in most cases, it affects the children adversely.
d. Single parenthood can be hard and lonely. The absence of an adult with whom you can share the burden of decision-making (particularly those affecting finances) and disciplining children makes life hard.
e. Dealing with the daddy question ("Why don't I have a dad?") or the mommy question ("When am I going to get a mum?") is another formidable challenge.
f. When you are forced to look for babysitters, neighbors, friends and family members to fall back on in times of emergency you may feel disadvantaged and start pitying yourself.
g. The society's perception that only children with two parents grow up to be responsible, productive citizens is a major challenge, as it may erode the self-confidence of your child, yourself or both.
h. Single parenthood is not always viewed positively by friends, family members and colleagues, and some may even stigmatize it.

Characteristics of Successful Single Parenthood
acceptance of responsibility

Successful single parents are those who accept the responsibility and challenges of single parenting. They neither minimize nor exaggerate problems but seek solutions instead. In addition, they learn to come to terms with challenges that go with single parenthood (such as reduced personal time, a restricted social life, sole responsibility for meeting multiple needs and financial stress) without self-pity or bitterness.

Commitment to family
Successful single parents make the family their highest priority. They focus on being the best possible single parents, which means addressing the needs of the child high in hierarchy of the things to do. They genuinely like and enjoy their children, sacrificing time, money and energy for their sake. They

try to be supportive and patient and help their children cope.They are consistent in disciplining the children.

Open Communication

Successful single parents foster open communication. They encourage clear and open expression of thoughts and feelings in the family as key to developing honest and trusting relationships.

Successful home management

Successful single parents strive to be well organized and dependable, and they work hard to coordinate schedules. They take pride in their abilityto provide financiallyfor the familydespite the fact that finances are usually a challenge.

Care of Self

Despite time limitation, successful single parents recognize the importance of personal care. This entails personal grooming, and intentionally seeking to have a healthy, spiritual, emotional and social life. Such people make sure they cultivate networks of people whom they can call upon for help and emotional support.

maintaining Traditions and relationships

These vary from family to family, and examples include praying together, participating in family get-togethers for special celebrations, visitations, celebrating birthdays, holding graduation parties for family members, among others. When the family togetherness has been disrupted, maintaining traditions becomes a stabilizing force, as it mitigates the sense of loss. If the other parent is still living, their involvement in observing the family traditions should be encouraged, so long as they do not present any danger to the child.

have a Positive Outlook on Changes

The successful single parent has a positive attitude towards parenting and sees positive aspects even in stressful situations and senses success despite the existence of doubt.

Tips for Single Parents

a. Help your children appreciate singlehood as a normal aspect of life
b. Find stable and safe child care
c. Establish a beneficial home routine and stick to it
d. Apply rules and discipline clearly and consistently
e. Allow your children to be children; do not ask them to deal with adult problems
f. Get to know the important people in your children's life
g. Answer questions about the other parent calmly and honestly
h. Avoid behavior that causes your children to feel pressed to choose between you or the other parent
i. Explain financial limitations honestly

Teenage Parenthood

Being a teen parent is difficult.During teenage,one experiences moral, spiritual, physical, social, mental, educational and career developmental milestones.Again,the individual is trying to find him/herself and at the same time create foundations. Becoming a teen parent places huge responsibilities on an individual who is yet to negotiate his/her own maturation.
Having a baby is *the biggest responsibility* any person can have in life. Henceforth, you are responsible not only for yourself but also for a dependent individual for more than eighteen years. Unsupported teenagers are more likely to have babies with health complications, such as low birth weight and prematurity. Getting extra support can thus help a teenage parent manage any academic or behavioral issues their children might have.AstudybyClaire,Simon,and Rosalind (2010) shows that if teenage parents get a chance to continue with their education, life will be easier for them and their children in the end.

Every woman upon learning that she is pregnant experiences various emotions, some positive (for example happiness and anticipation), and others negative (for example anxiety and doubt). Some get confused or fragmented; some tend to ignore the symptoms in the hope that they will disappear. Most teenagers are afraid of informing their parents or guardians, uncertain about where to get help and support. Such may find themselves contending with questions such as, how will my family react? Will the baby's father help me? Do we love each other? Should we get married? What will my parents-in-law be like? What will characterize the pregnancy? Will the baby be alright? Who will pay the expenses? Will I be able to finish school? How will my life turn out to be? It is therefore advisable that a teenager, upon learning that they are pregnant, talk to someone they trust as soon as possible. Such a person could be a doctor, a nurse, a parent, a counselor, a pastor, a social worker or a family planning counselor.

Concerns about Teenage Parents

A high percentage of teenage mothers are unmarried and many may never get married. Babies born of teenagers have a higher risk of serious health problems. Teenagers who become pregnant and drop out of school are not likely to return to school. As a result, they face life without skills that can get them jobs and this may make them remain financially dependent on their families.

Health Risks Associated with Teenage Pregnancy

Adolescent pregnancy poses health risks for both the mother and child, since the mother's body is not mature. Schilmoeller, Baranowski, and Higgins (1991) argue that as a result, the expectant teenager may experience complications during pregnancy, for instance, induced hypertension and even if she manages a full-term pregnancy, her birth canal may be too small for the passage of a full term baby.

In my counselling with girls who contend with teenage pregnancy, I have realized they hardly attend prenatal care though they seriously require it because of their high-risk status brought about by conceiving when they are still developing physically. During the counselling sessions, I inform them they need to have regular pre-natal care during early months as well as later months of pregnancy.

Challenges of Teenage Pregnancy

A teenager who becomes pregnant is exposed to the following challenges:
a. Lack of maturity exposes her to health risks
b. Having a baby to look after means loss of independence
c. Pregnancy may mean dropping out of school
d. Her social life is affected
e. The need for medical attention while pregnant and demands of the baby

exposes her to financial challenges.

f. Her short and long term goals are affected

grandparents raising grandchildren

Grandparents raising grandchildren is becoming a common phenomenon in Kenya. This has been necessitated by diverse factors including children giving birth when they are under-age and having to go back to school, death of parents, relocation of parents, parents having chronic illnesses, separation and divorce of parents and parents abandoning their children. When parents are absent or unable to raise their children, grandparents are often the ones who step in. Taking another round of parenting means that you have to reorient yourself again to the art of parenting. You may probably have forgotten many things related to childcare and there may be contemporary changes regarding childcare you may have to contend with. You will have to do a lot of learning and adjustments to parent effectively. Your grandchildren too will benefit immensely from receiving parenting from someone they can trust.

The Case of Hamza

Hamza grew up under the guardianship of his grandmother who loved, cared and protected him. He was a third born in his mother's family whom he came to know as his mother when he was 21 years. He had always thought she was a visitor who came occasionally. She could bring another younger child whenever she came. Hamza treasured sitting in the kitchen to listen to his grandma's hilarious stories.

One day, Hamza asked his grandmother why his mother did not visit them often. She looked at him in the eye and said, "She will come one of these fine days.She works far off and she is not able to come."She drew near to Hamza and lovingly told him, "While mum is away, I will take care of all of you so that you will lack nothing. I am a capable custodian who will rear you to become a capable, respectable man." From then on Hamza became secure and happier with the knowledge that his grandma would always be there for him. However, he never developed an attachment with his mother. Even now, she is a stranger to him and he hardly knows what to talk about with her. She tries to be close but he always keeps a distance asking himself,"Why does she need me now? Does she visit because I have become successful in spite of her negligence?"

From Hamza's case, you can imagine that Hamza would have lived a neglected life if the grandmother did not take up the responsibility. It would seem the grandmother was cautious not to give Hamza negative stories regarding his mother. She knew that would devastate the child hence she was tight lipped about it. She presumed a biological mother can never be replaced and she would always be grandma playing a mother's role. She devotedly provided counsel, friendship, love and basic needs to the child. Hamza was assured that all his needs would be taken care of and grandma had big dreams for Hamza, which later materialized.

How Can Grandparents Parent Grandchildren Skillfully

Deal with Internal Resistance
My mother in law has brought up three of my youngest sister in law's children. My sister in law, now married, lacked the means to bring up her children though she really wanted to take charge as a parent. She was second last in a family of eleven children and it seems like my parents in law had relaxed their parenting grip when it came to the last set of their children. She did not pursue education and she was reserved in ways that limited her. She was a single parent and was largely unprepared for the dynamic responsibility of parenthood. She struggled seriously to provide them with upkeep and eventually my mother in law had to take up the role.

My mother in law clearly had mixed feelings about taking up the children. On one hand, she had a strong feeling it was not her duty but on the other hand, parenting them was giving her company, people to help her with chores and give her purpose in life. They made her spring back to life though she resented having to parent a second time. Incidentally, she loved those children very much and devoted herself to parenting them to the best of her ability. However, she complained a lot that my sister in law was not appreciative of her kind gesture. She could taunt her and at times make statements that made her daughter feel disowned and somehow cursed. I used to ask my mother in law what was pushing her to that level of frustration and she could say the daughter was not appreciative.

Admittedly, there are mixed feelings that come with parenting someone else's child. There are many reasons that can put a grandmother in a position of parenting again. From watching my mother in law parent her grandchildren, I appreciated it is natural to feel conflicted when parenting children who are not legitimately yours.

If you are parenting your grandchildren,it is not initially easy to embrace the task. There are many children brought up by their grandmothers and they are very balanced individuals who are high achievers in family, work and social life. As a grandmother, you are removing a child from a situation of neglect and abandonment to give them a new lease of life. You therefore have to work through your internal conflicts related to taking up the responsibility of parenting your grandchild.

Nurture Yourself
When you were younger, you perhaps did not expect to be raising kids again at this stage in your life. At times, the physical, emotional, and financial demands may be overwhelming.It is therefore important that you mind your health and seek the support you need. When you are preoccupied with the daily demands of raising grandchildren, it is easy to forget you also require nurture. Remember, taking care of 'you' is a necessity, not a luxury. You cannot be a good custodian when you are perpetually overwhelmed, exhausted, and emotionally depleted. In order to keep up with the demands of your grandchildren, you need to be calm and focused, and this stable state is achieved after you have been taking care of your own mental and physical health. The following are ways you can take care of yourself:

a. Accepting that this has happened to you and choose to enjoy it b. Deal with conflictual thoughts and feelings regarding the new state of affairs

c. Talk about your struggles to a counsellor to help you deal with unresolved issues
d. Look for another grandmother in similar circumstances who seems comfortable with the role and let this person support you through the transition period

Plan for Your Grandchild's Financial Needs
Within the Kenyan context, this is the most vexing aspect for grandmothers parenting grandchildren. This is because you are grand parenting when you

may not have the energies to earn enough revenue to take care of all your grandchild's needs. You may also have retired from salaried employment and therefore you do not have a steady source of income.You have to lookfor ways to supplement your finances to take care of your grandchildren. This mostly happens if the child's parents for whatever reason are not supporting the child financially. The following can be useful:

a. Asking your other grown up children to support you in ways they can manage. They can make it a key agenda in their meetings.
b. You can also ask well-wishers to give financial support towards this venture
c. You can start a money making project to take care of the emerging needs of the child: upkeep, schooling, medical and personal effects
d. You can also approach funding organizations like Constituency Development Fund, churches, local NGOs, FBOs and CBOs and other organizations that deal with sponsorship. However, conduct thorough background checks on such organizations/ individuals to ensure the child's safety

Help your Grandchild Deal with Changes in Parenting
Being parented by a grandparent is not easy for any child. The child will inherently ask questions about his/her biological parent's failure to parent him/her. Therefore, it will take time for your grandchild to adjust, and in the meantime, he/she may act in unexpected ways and seem ungrateful. Moreover, if the child has suffered from emotional neglect, trauma, or abuse, those wounds will not immediately disappear just because he/she is now in a safe place. To help your grandchild resolve emerging issues surrounding being parented by a grandparent, you can:
a. Book the child for counselling to deal with his/her internal

conflicts and frustrations
b. Let the child know he/she can talk about his/her troubles to you.You should be a confidant to the child
c. Look for a mentor who can be there for the child if he/she wants to talk out frustrations
d. Encourage the child to write down his/her frustrations and to read them out to you

e. Let the child keep contact with the biological parents and
facilitate moments for meeting and talking
f. Get a teacher who can support the child in school/academic
matters
g. Celebrate and praise the child when he/she does well in certain
things; this will be a confidence booster

Create a Secure Environment for the Child
If a grandchild is moving to your home to stay there, prepare for his/ her
arrival and make necessary adjustments to meet his/her needs. Set apart a
place for him/her to sleep; this space should feel personal for the child. Let
your grandchild notice you are putting effort to accommodate him/her. This
way, your grandchild will feel accepted in the new environment and will start
settling down even emotionally. Please remember children thrive in an
environment that is stable and predictable. Therefore,

a. Prepare a ceremony to welcome your grandchild to the new home
b. Introduce your grandchild to the rest of the family members
c. Handle any fears the child may have
d. Set up routines of activities he/she will be involved in. Let him/ her know
it is important to corporate with others in the home
e. Let your grandchild know it's okay to feel low in the beginning; but this
feeling will dissipate as he/she gets used to the new environment
f. Where necessary, teach the child how to perform certain tasks and
supervise to ensure they are carried out thoroughly

Plan for Celebration Moments for the Child
Plan for occasions when others can celebrate your grandchild. Such moments
may include birthdays and graduation days. Make it routine to celebrate your
grandchild's achievements; this makes him/her develop a sense of being
valued and confidence. During these celebration moments, significant others
can interact with the child for inspiration.

Evolving Parenthoods
lesbian and gay Parented Children

In Kenya, lesbianism and gayism is largely unaccepted, though it is a reality
kept away from significant others. Moreover, lesbian and gay parenting is

unheard of in our setting since Kenyan laws and conventional values do not allow lesbian and gay marriages. President Obama on 25 July 2015 made a plea for protection of gay rights during his visit to Kenya, warning that bad things happen when countries discriminate against certain groups of people. In response, President Kenyatta rejoined, *"For Kenyans today, the issue of gay rights is really a non-issue. We want to focus on other areas that affect day-to-day living of our people."* The religious institutions have been outraged against the increasingly growing trend of homosexuality. In Kenya currently, homosexuality is a banned lifestyle that many consider to be shrouded with mystery.

Martin (1998) says, "lesbian and gay parented families, where they exist, are a function of two things: one is the rich variety of family constellations they comprise, and the other is the fact that they exist in a society which does not yet value rich variety. The tension created by this situation hence generates unique needs for gay and lesbian parents whenever they present themselves to the legal system, the educational system, the mental health profession, religious organizations, the medical profession, or the insurance industry."

Martin (1998) reckons that the ability of lesbian and gay parents to provide just as adequately as heterosexual parents for the social and emotional health of their children has been riddled with controversy, even elsewhere in the world. Saying that these children are like other children from heterosexual parents is a refusal to scrutinize the impact deeply.

impact of gay and lesbian Parenting on Children's development In some of my counseling sessions,I have listened to enough testimonies of those who desire this kind of family arrangement and I now know we cannot ignore its impact. I believe the 21st century realities have to be contended with directly rather than wishing them away. Though this family arrangement may appear to be far removed from our context, we have few cases that would benefit from this discussion. Discussed hereafter are some challenges that befall children of lesbian and gay parents. This is not to mean that children of heterosexual parents do not suffer the same problems but their intensity maybe different.

Discrimination
Children from gay and lesbian households have to put up with labeling and

stigma related with the sexual orientation of their parents and this can be very overwhelming for them. Such children develop shame linked with their parent's lifestyle but they are not able to express their misgivings. They therefore internalize their embarrassment thus becoming shame based. This affects the children's relationship with themselves and other people due to low self-worth.

Chronic Secrecy

In an environment where gayism and lesbianism is openly rebuffed, it is difficult for individuals to come out of the closet for fear of being ostracized. Hence, they keep their experiences tacked away lest they are defamed by others. Children in such families are caught up in this situation where some issues are swept under the carpet. As a result, they also become secretive and are not open to their experiences. This status quo makes them ordinarily develop mental health problems, which would interfere with their wholesome lifestyle.

Identity Issues

When one's identity is not clearly defined, it interferes with one's approach to life's issues. Children define themselves based on the modeling of their parents. They are able to allow their maleness and femaleness to emerge onlyif there are adult figures who are facilitating that. Children in gay and lesbian parents may not complete the task of defining who theyare because of the secrecyassociated to the lifestyle. This may make them experience a sense of incompleteness regarding their sexuality.

Lack of Legal Recognition

Lack of legal recognition of lesbian and gay marriages is likely to affect a child immensely like in a case of two lesbian or gay parents. This is due to the fact that one parent will not have legal ownership of the child. This means the child would not benefit fully from both parents. For example, insurance may also refuse to cover the child of a non-legal parent. This can make a child feel disadvantaged, different from other children in a negative sense and ultimately rejected. This eventually affects a child's sense of trust, belongingness and security in the family.

Janice's Case
Janice, a sister of a gay man (Ben), agreed to become pregnant as a

The case of Janice illuminates the complicated nature of relationships in gay and lesbian families. If not handled well, these dynamics can make children develop intense internal conflicts and personality disorders, which would hurt their growth.

Polyamorous Parenting

The Oxford Dictionary describes polyamory as the practice of engaging in multiple sexual relationships with the consent of all the people involved. It is regulated by a set rules and regulations that define the practice. The term polyamory is derived from the Greek words 'poly' (many or multiple) and 'amor' (love). Polyamory does not refer solely to people who are polyamorous but rather describes the philosophy of many 'loves' as opposed to monogamous relationships. Polyamory also refers to the concept of consensual non-monogamy.

Polyamory can take many forms, from multiple people living together and sharing day-to-day life or it could involve an individual dating multiple people with no intention of settling down with anyone. It could be a primary couple who each have other relationships, together or separately or perhaps it is an interconnected network of people who are involved with each other.

This practice of polyamory parenting is becoming quite common in Kenya especially among the elite and affluent persons.However,there is a lot of secrecy regarding polyamory relationships since it is still not accepted in the Kenyan society. I have included this section so that it can inform those in polyamory practice about how their own children may get affected by their relationship choices.

Dr. Karen Ruskin, a marriage and family therapist in United States (2010) offers that some people who are in polyamorous relationships truly believe it is a grand thing while they are in it. Certainly, there are aspects of polyamory that are indeed grand for them. In my counseling experience with polyamorous individuals, I pick intense, mixed feelings and thoughts arising from the lifestyle. On one hand, most feel content and satisfied with the plural romantic relationships while on the other hand they seem clouded and unhappy when they think about their lifestyle. They want to keep aspects of their relationship private to their parents, friends and children. Most fear these significant others would be devastated if they knew the truth. They also confess to not feeling spiritual enough and they refrain from spiritual engagements because they do not feel holy enough to approach God.

Kanya and Norman's Case
Kanya has never enjoyed sexual fulfillment from Norman, though she has always pressurized him for it. When she was in primary school, she realized she was unusually attracted to other girls with whom she ended up having lesbian relationships.

After basic schooling, she went to a college where she performed exceptionally well in her studies. She later married and they got three male children. In her tenth year of marriage, she asked her spouse whether he could entertain polyamory marriage, and he readily accepted. She soon hit it off with Corazon who was also in polyamory, and the two families got really engaged with each other, with the children having more extended deep relationships with other adults and their children. Since then, Kanya and Norman have been having other romantic relationships, which are guided by strict rules. Their children are adolescents now and they have become aware of their parents' lifestyles. As a result, they are shattered by shame and confusion emanating from what they consider uncommon relationships.

Kanya and Norman seem to have normalized their multipronged romantic relationships and are oblivious of their children's struggles. While they are contented with their lifestyles, their children are suffering helplessly. Undoubtedly, these children from their testimonies will be dented for life unless they decide to salvage themselves by resolving these issues and redefining themselves.

Characteristics of Children Parented by Polyamory Couples When children live in perpetual fear of losing valued relationships, this

does not foreshadow a healthy life for the child. Children internalize fear of the unknown regarding relationships and they develop intense mistrust. Ruskin (2014) argues that children living in such an arrangement may have a hard time giving and receiving love when they grow up, having been negatively affected by this lifestyle. To such children, there is no permanency in relationships. They do not imagine any relationship can be stable to the extent of lasting a lifetime.

In my counseling experience, I have observed that children from polyamorous marriages tend to be unduly private, particularly on matters to do with the family. Such family secrets or skeletons in the closet affect the children who are supposed to keep them, as they grow older. Having to keep a secret about something that is not accepted by society may lead to emotional hurt as the child grows. It is an unnecessary burden on their part.

Children of parents in polyamorous relationships are often forced to keep the secret from their friends so that no one views them negatively. Even when their parents allow them to open up, they are not able to do so for fear of rejection. By keeping the information private, they try to protect themselves from society's onslaught on them and their family.

impact of Polyamory on Children
Ruskin (2014) lists the following as some behavioral tendencies children develop when they grow up in a polyamory family arrangement:

a. *They are over sensitive to their mate's friendships.* Often, they become controlling regarding the kind of friendships their partner should have and are particularly opposed to their having friends of the opposite gender.

b. *They have the I-will-break-up-with-you-before-you-break-up-withme mentality.* There are those who are consciously aware of their intentions to sabotage the relationship but press ahead with their decision to protect their interests. The reason behind this callousness is the deep hurt they experienced during their childhood, and which they determine to avoid at all costs in their adulthood.

c. *They shield themselves from being injured by others.* They tell themselves, *"If I only guard my territory, I will never be hurt."* This is the way the child who is used to love coming in and going out of their life through significant adult figures reasons in their subconscious.

d. *They easily sabotage relationships and* when they break up with a person because of something bad that they have done, they blame the action that has ended the relationship instead of their bad attitude that makes them difficult to cope with.

e. *Their relationships are characterized by dependence.*Their longing for a long-term, consistent relationship is so powerful that they cling helplessly to friends in the hope that this will make the persons not leave because you need them.

It is important to point out that polyamorous families do not benefit the children but the adults in those relationships. In my counselling with such children, it has become apparent that they crave for relationships that make them feel more honored and respected. This in turn helps them develop their own integrity and honor. When parents' behaviors are informed by the desire for self-gratification,they rob children their self-respect, and children feel abandoned and ashamed of themselves.

Such children need other individuals or institutions to mentor them and help them define their values. They should know they can heal themselves by acknowledging their limits, that is, they cannot order their parents on how they should behave, but they can decide to live lives that honor them.

Adrian's Story
Adrian says, "Surely we children of parents in open or polyamorous relationships are never the beneficiaries of those relationships. I believe that parents get into them due to their own self-seeking needs. I am 35, and this is the time I am starting to feel confident to open up and think logically about what I felt and thought regarding my parents' 'love life' growing up. When I was much younger, I could not figure out what was happening but in my early adolescence, I started realizing that my parent's relationships were indeed queer. I had come to know that the parents of my friends were not behaving like my parents. They were decent, controlled and responsible. My parents on the other hand were oblivious of how we felt regarding their extreme fun life.

They were so consumed in their joys and highs to notice our struggles. I started developing a sense of deep shame, inferiority and insecurity; and I could notice the same in my siblings. I kind of figured my parents had reached a point they didn't care and they didn't want to know. Now, my mother is 63 and I asked her the other day whether she thought about how their lifestyle was impacting us and she said she didn't really think about it but she secretly hoped I wouldn't tell and knew I wouldn't. She described the most "open" period of their marriage as being outside of herself looking in, much like an addict. I told her how hurt we were when they brought in their lovers for a sleep over in our place over the weekends. We didn't know what to feel and think about the whole bunch of them as they changed their lovers like clothes. Life revolved around them and we were the spectators of the most heinous acts meted on children. I am the person I am today despite them, not because of them.

Going to church when I was young helped me develop pure values but the sense of betrayal remained. All of these websites singing praises of such marriages are just nauseating. Parents need to be honorable, dignified and morally responsible adults to their children. It's hard enough being a parent and a spouse to one set of kids and one spouse. When you bring another love interest into your marriage, finding time is even harder. The children are the ones that suffer, always! I hear statements that children suffer when their parent's lovers leave; I never felt any love or closeness to them. I detested them and was resentful to my parents. I still struggle with these feelings terribly."

Adrian's testimony brings out the corrosiveness, ugliness and absurdity of polyamorous relationships to children. He says he has estranged relationships with his parents whom he considered to have been unacceptably selfish. He resents such relationships and intensely believes that parents should be trustworthy and be thoughtful about their children in all their actions. It is interesting that the church helped Adrian develop values that were acceptable to him. This helps us appreciate that such children in open marriages need mentoring from responsible individuals or institutions to help them define their values and grow in healthy ways.

Parenting Across Different Ages

Chapter 3

ChaPTEr ThrEE
ParENTiNg aCrOSS diffErENT agES

*"Embrace your beautiful mess of a life with your child. No matter how hard it gets, do not disengage... Do something—anything—to connect with and guide your child today. Parenting is an adventure of the greatest significance. It is your legacy."***andy Kerckhoff**

Parenting children across different developmental stages requires unique knowledge, attitude and skills. It is the process of ingraining the necessary software for effective living in a lifecycle. Our children, Kenna and Keega are in their late adolescence and when I look back, I realize we have had to learn how to parent them properly in every developmental stage; instilling the relevant abilities, capacities and knowledge needed at each phase. You are certainly going through the same sprints as you parent your children. Learning how to parent NEVER ends. You as a parent should be an eager student of parenting, all the time learning different capabilities, knowhow and realities about parenting.

Children have different developmental needs as they grow from one stage to another. Your role as a parent is to appreciate these needs and respond to them appropriately. Therefore, your parental skills and methods have to resonate with your child's growth needs, making parental training essential to facilitate your ability to parent your child at different stages of growth. The worst you can do to your child is to parent your child ignorantly; it is very costly in a negative sense. Skills acquired by children, such as taking a first step, smiling for the first time, and waving bye-bye are called developmental milestones. Developmental milestones are abilities most children achieve by a certain age.At particular times, children are able to do certain things for example to sit, crawl, stand, run, sing and recite, jump, feed themselves and tell stories. As a parent, you naturally get fretful if your child does not pick abilities at the same age as his/her peers. However, you should resolve this anxiety lest you project it on your child thus affecting him/ her more.

infants (The first year)

Kail (2011) offers that in the first year,babies learn to focus their vision, reach out, explore, and learn about the things that are around them. Kail further says learning the language is more than making sounds ("babble"), or saying "ma-ma" and "da-da." Listening, understanding, and knowing the names of people and things are all a part of language development. Erik Erikson (1950), the father of psychosocial development explains that during this stage, babies are also developing bonds of love and trust with their parents and others as part of social and emotional development. The way you cuddle, hold, and play with your baby will set the basis for how he/she will interact and socialize. What babies learn in socialization is what they internalize and use spontaneously.

Children from the time they start moving need to know what is harmful and dangerous for them. When you have small children, make sure your home is safe. Look around your home for things that could be dangerous to your baby and make sure they are out of the baby's reach. As a parent, it is your job to ensure that you create a safe home for your baby. It also is important that you take the necessary steps to make sure that you are mentally and emotionally ready for your new baby. If you are not emotionally and mentally ready, this can affect your care and ability to be flexible to accommodate the child. In some worse situations, this unpreparedness leads to depression.

Safety and health measures for Parenting an infant
Safety Health

a) Guarantee your child's caregiver is somebody with ability to take care of a small child. Teach her essentials to enable her take care of your baby. Make sure you confirm the identity of this care giver to ascertain the kind of a person he/she is

a) Breast milk meets all your baby's needs for the first 6 months. Between 6 and 12 months, your baby will learn new tastes and textures of healthy, solid food, but breast milk should still be an important source of nutrition

b) Do not leave your child with things he/she can put in the mouth. Babies can easily swallow items and this can be fatal

c) Never shake a baby. Babies have very weak neck muscles that are not yet able to support their heads. If you shake your baby, you can damage the brain or even cause death

d) Make sure you always put your baby to sleep on his/her back to prevent sudden infant death

e) Protect your baby and family from second-hand smoke. Do not allow anyone to smoke in your home

f) Prevent your baby from choking by cutting food into small pieces. Also, don't let the baby play with small toys and other things that might be easy to swallow

g) Don't allow your baby to play with anything that might cover his/her face
b) Feed your baby slowly and

patiently. Encourage him/her to try new tastes, but do not force. Watch closely to note when the baby is satisfied

c) Breastfeeding is the natural way to feed your baby, but it can be challenging because you need to feed well and be available

d) Keep your baby active. While the baby might not be able to run and play like the older children just yet, there's a lot he/she can do to keep the little arms and legs moving. Even crawling on the floor helps your baby become strong, learn, and explore

e) Do not to keep your baby in swings, strollers, bouncer seats, and exercise saucers for too long

f) Regulate TV watching time h) Never carry hot liquids or foods near your baby or while holding him/her.
Kail (2011)

i) Vaccines (shots) are important to protect your child's health and ensure safety. Because children can get serious diseases, it is important that your child gets the right shots at the right time. Talk with your child's doctor to make sure your child is up-to-date in terms of vaccinations

Laura (2012)

Advice for Parenting Infants a. Try as much as you can to be available for your child; this facilitates healthy bonding.

b. Be happy around your child to help him/her generate positivity and natural happiness.

c. Talk to your child and help him/her articulate words clearly. Repeat words and phrases until the child gets them like 'mum' 'mum' 'dad' 'dad.'

d. When your child is scared, hold him/her close to yourself so that he/she can develop trust and security.

e. Attend to your child's needs like feeding, changing diapers, holding him/her when he/she cries. The child learns from this age, he/she is esteemed and prized.

f. Play with the child by introducing different play materials to facilitate the child to interact through play.

g. Teach your child the vital abilities like laughter, sitting, crawling, standing, walking, and being gentle.

h. Protect your child against any form of abuse or neglect. This makes a child start developing negativity from an early age.

Toddlers (1-2 years)

Children at this age have learnt to stand, run and move around more

with lots of excitement. Sharman, Cross and Vennis (2004) argue that these children are aware of themselves and their surroundings. Their desire for adventure is seen in their curiosity for new territories and wanting to hold, touch and manipulate things. They find the world to be mesmerizing and they are all ready to learn. Henceforth, during this stage, toddlers will show greater independence, begin to show defiant behavior,recognize themselves in pictures or in the mirror; and imitate the behavior of others, especially adults and older children. Toddlers should also be able to recognize the names of familiar people and objects, form simple phrases and sentences, and follow simple instructions.

Safety and health measures for Parenting Toddlers
Safety Health

a) Do not leave your toddler near or around water (for example, bathtubs, pools, ponds, lakes, or the ocean) without someone watching him/her. Fence off backyard pools. Drowning is the leading cause of injury and death among children of this age

a) Give your child water and plain milk instead of sugary drinks. Even after the first year when your growing toddler is eating more and different solid foods, breast milk is still an ideal addition to his/her diet

b) Block off stairs with a small gate or fence. Lock doors to dangerous places, such as the garage or basement

c) Ensure that your home is toddler-proof by placing plug covers on all electrical outlets when they are not in use

d) Keep kitchen appliances, iron boxes and heaters out of the reach of your toddler. Turn pot handles toward the back of the stove

b) Your toddler might become a very picky and erratic eater. Toddlers need less food in their second year because they are growing more slowly. They have small stomachs so should need to eat small amounts often. It is best not to battle with him/ her over this. Offer a selection of healthy foods and let him/ her choose what he/she wants. Keep trying new foods; it might take time for him/her to learn to like them

c) Limit TV watching time

e) Keep sharp objects such as scissors, knives, and pens in a safe place

f) Lock up medicines, household cleaners, and poisons
d) Your toddler will seem to be

moving continually – running, kicking, climbing, or jumping. Let him/her be active; he/she is developing his/her coordination and becoming strong

Kail (2011)
g) Do not leave your toddler alone in any vehicle (car, truck, van) even for a few minutes

h) Store any weapon in a safe place, out of your child's reach.
Laura (2012)

advice for Parenting Toddlers

a. Be a friend to your child by responding to his/her needs. These include eating, toileting, talking and removing clothes.

b. Teach your child abilities like toilet procedures, dressing, feeding and climbing places safely. They are overly eager to learn and their memory retention of learning is very high. Children at this age are very excited at new learning and it gives them confidence in themselves.

c. Help to develop your toddler's language skills by talking with him/her and assist in completing words or phrases he/she is trying to utter. For example, if your toddler says "baba", you can respond, "Yes, you are right, that is a bottle."

d. Provide age appropriate learning materials for the child. e. Teach discipline by rewarding and appreciating your child's good behavior and pointing out or punishing bad behavior.
Appreciation is known to help in instilling good behavior than punishment.
f. Engage them in play; this facilitates development of positive temperaments.
g. Children at this age can become increasingly aggressive; help them control their emotions through gently talking to them and allowing them to express their frustrations verbally. h. Introduce pictures, objects and images to them so that they can develop their language further by naming those pictures, objects and images.
i. Help your child to start developing his/her attention span by appreciating the expanded attention span in carrying out activities.

Early Childhood (Preschoolers) (3-5 years)
As children grow into early childhood, their world begins to open up. They become more independent since they are able to do various things for themselves.They become more confident in dealing with what they are exposed to. They are also very adventurous and they can easily get lost in crowded areas. You need to be sure of where they are. They have a bigger capacity of grasping information and you should teach them on distinguishing safe and dangerous persons and what they can do in case they encounter dangerous persons. Their interactions with family members and those around them will help shape their personality and their ways of thinking and interrelating. During this stage, children are able to do various activities like cleaning themselves after they go to the toilet, dress and undress themselves, engage in productive play, tell stories, sing and dance.

Safety and health measures for Parenting Preschoolers
Safety Health

a) Tell your child why it is important to stay out of traffic. Note that children are fun loving and they can be oblivious of lurking dangers. Tell him/her not to play in the street or run after stray balls

a) Eat meals with your child whenever possible. Let your child see you enjoying fruits, vegetables, and whole grains at meals and snacks. Your child should eat and drink only a limited amount of food and beverages that contain added sugars, solid fats, or salt

b) Be cautious when letting your child ride his/her
bicycle. Keep him/her on the sidewalk and away from the street and always have him/ her wear a helmet

b) Limit TV watching time for your child to no more than 1 hour per day of quality programs at home, school, or elsewhere where there is reliable child care

c) Check outdoor playground equipment to make sure there are no loose parts or sharp edges
c) Provide your child with age
appropriate play equipment, like balls and plastic bats, but let your preschooler choose what to play. This makes moving and being active fun for your preschooler

d) Watch your child at all times, especially when he/ she is playing outside. If you are not available, leave your child with a trusted person to take care of him/her

e) Teach safety in the water. Teach your child to swim, but watch him/her at all times when he/she is in or around any body of water (this includes children pools)

f) Teach your child how to be Kail (2011)
safe around strangers

Marian's Case
Marian's parents had stayed for seven years without a child. They were blessed with wealth and they were very generous to needy people in their neighborhood. So, the neighborhood was overjoyed when Peter and Mary got Marian. Marian at four years loved playing near the pool with Nicky, her dog. One sunny morning, she pleaded with her aunt to allow her play near the pool. The aunt was very stern and warned Marian to stay away from the pool. She ran off laughing heartily; after some time, the aunt could not hear the usual noises and she ran out only to find Marian's body floating on the water and Nicky looking at the waters.

Marian's parents may have coached Marian's aunt on rules and regulations the young child needed to follow in the compound, and especially around the swimming pool. However, they had not fenced off the swimming pool and this caused the death of their only child. As a parent, make sure you are not leaving any gaps or chances that can present risk for your growing child.

advice on Parenting Preschoolers

a. Support your child's independence by encouraging age appropriate tasks and activities like simple home chores like cleaning (plates, cups and spoons), cleaning parts of the house and removing items like utensils to the kitchen.

b. Teach your child good manners at this stage. Children who are left on their own regarding right and wrong at this stage grow up as "naughty brats." It is rather difficult to change their ways after this age; hence, this is the right time to ingrain morality around general aspects of life like not fighting, biting others, insulting, throwing things at others and urinating on others.

c. Continue teaching self-care behaviors like dressing, removing clothes, eating, hand washing, bathing, putting dirty clothes in designated places and covering themselves neatly when they sleep. A key hygiene behavior for girls is to teach them how to wipe themselves after visiting the toilet; girls should wipe from front to back; back to front exposes a girl to infections due to feces that can be deposited in the vagina.

d. Children at this age are in baby and nursery classes in Kenya. You should buy them stage appropriate learning materials with illustrations so that they can clearly understand through pictorials what you want them to learn.

e. Encourage your child to play with other children. Play helps them bond with others and create friendships that enhance their growth and development.

f. Continue expanding their language base through pictures, images, items, recitations, poems, songs and reading.

g. Children this age are continuing to learn the world through curiosity and adventure. They can therefore harm themselves, harm others or damage things. They like touching things and picking things; however, due to inexperience they can be hurt in the end. Picture a child who wants to grab flames of fire or hold a laser blade with his/her palm.

h. Discipline is essential for these children since they are very selfish and impulsive.They believe everything belongs to them and therefore they demand what they desire. Imagine being with your son in a supermarket and he starts throwing tantrums demanding a big toy vehicle. You can almost sense everyone stealing glances at you. One audacious shopper may tell you to talk to your child and another may suggest that you buy the boy what he wants. You are visibly embarrassed and irritated. You then remember you had agreed with him before you got into the supermarket that you were only going to pick a few things since you did not have money. You hold both his hands and mutter,"Son, I will definitely buy you the big toy, but not today, you remember our agreement?" He reluctantly answers, "Yes mum." After saying that, he walks away dejected but calmer. You are glad you remained calm and persistent.

i. Children at this stage require basic life skills like relating and dealing with dangerous relationships. For example, your child should know he/she should not eat foods given by strangers or follow strangers. You should take your child through drills to teach such lessons.

j. Give your child a limited number of simple choices (for example, deciding what to wear, when to play, and what to eat)

middle Childhood (6-8 years)

Middle childhood brings many changes in a child's life. During this time, children are able to undertake more activities and assume more responsibility. Their personality starts to emerge more distinctly. You may realize your child is an extrovert (outgoing) or introvert (reserved). Having independence from family becomes more important now. Events such as starting school bring children this age into regular contact with the larger world. Friendships become more and more important in helping them expand their capacity. Physical, social, and mental skills develop quickly at this time. This is a critical time for children to develop confidence in different areas of life through friends, schoolwork, and sports.

Emotional and Social Development
Thinking and Learning
Children in this age group might:
a) Have ability to

manage their emotions much better

b) Show ability to take care of others especially children younger than them

c) Display higher ability of relating with friends and interact in better ways

d) Undertake activities alongside other persons with
respectable levels of competence

e) Exhibit
extraordinary interest in
social activities like singing,
recitation, drama and cleaning
the environment alongside other children

Children in this age group might:
a) Think with clarity and explain situations and issues with a relatively higher level of rationality

b) Learn better ways to describe experiences and talk about thoughts and feelings

c) Have less focus on themselves and more concern for others
Sharman, Cross, and Vennis (2004)

Safety and health measures for middle Childhood Parenting
Safety Health

More physical ability and more
independence can put children at risk of injuries from falls and other accidents. Motor vehicle crashes
are the most common cause of death from unintentional injury among children this age. Hence,

a) Explain to your child how to engage in any new situation so that he/she can feel empowered

b) Teach your child to watch out for traffic and how to be safe when walking to school, riding a bike,
and playing outdoors

c) Make sure your child understands water safety, and always supervise him/her when swimming or
playing near water

d) Supervise your child when he/she is engaged in risky activities, such as climbing

e) Talk with your child about how to ask for help when he/she needs it. Helping him/her know people
he/she can call in case of an emergency is essential

f) Keep potentially harmful household products, tools, equipment, and firearms out of your child's
reach. Even so, explain reasons he/she should not tamper with them.

Sharman, Cross, and Vennis

(2004)
a) Parents can help make
schools healthier. Work with your child's school to limit access to foods and drinks with added sugar,
solid fat, and salt that can be purchased outside the school lunch program

b) Make sure your child has 1 hour or more of physical activity each day

c) Limit TV watching time for your child to no more than 1 hour per day of quality programs at home,
school, or after school

d) Practice healthy eating habits and physical activity early. Encourage active play, and be a role model
by eating healthy at family mealtimes and by having an active lifestyle

Kail (2011)

advice on middle Childhood Parenting

Kail (2011) and Marilyn (1998) suggests the following activities to be

crucial in facilitating growth:

a. Show affection towards your child and celebrate his/her achievements

b. Help your child develop a sense of responsibility – ask him/her to help with household tasks, such as passing a cup to another person, setting the table or helping needy children

c. Talk with your child about school, friends, and things he/she looks forward to in the future. This helps your child listen to him/herself hence, develop more confidence

d. Talk with your child about respecting others through respectful talking and reference to others

e. Help your child set his/her own achievable goals and steps to achieving those goals

f. Help your child learn patience by letting others go first or by finishing a task before going out to play.Encourage him/her to think about possible consequences before acting

g. Make clear rules and stick to them, such as how long your child can watch TV or when he/she has to go to bed. Be clear about what behavior is okay and what is not okay. This helps your child develop internal limits through defining personal values

h. Engage in activities that make you bond like house work, family business, attending social and recreational activities

i. Get involved with your child's school. Meet the teachers and staff and get to understand their learning goals and how you and the school can work together to help your child do well

j. Use discipline to guide and protect your child, rather than punishment to make him/her feel bad about him/herself. Follow up any discussion about what *not* to do with a discussion of what *to* do instead

k. Praise your child for good behavior. It is best to focus praise more on what your child does ("You worked hard to figure this out") than on traits he/she can't change ("You are smart")

l. Support your child in taking on new challenges. Encourage him/ her to solve problems, such as a disagreement with another child, on his/her own

m. Encourage and support your child to join clubs, societies and other social groups. This helps the child develop relevant life skills for coexistence and honing interpersonal skills

late Childhood (9-11 years)

As your child enters the 9 to 11 age bracket, he/she will experience growth spurts at different rates that moves him/her towards adolescence. Typically, girls will begin to grow and mature faster than boys during this time. Children this age are more inclined to wanting to be independent but there is also noticeable peer pressure. Enabling relationships are vital for personality development and therefore encouraging healthy relationships is important. Children who feel good about themselves are more able to resist negative peer pressure and make better choices for themselves. Children at this age could be lured to having sex, help your child develop healthy values regarding his/her sexuality. This is an important time for children to gain a sense of responsibility along with their growing freedom.

Emotional and Social Development Thinking and Learning

Children in this age group might:
a) Start becoming aware they are now 'big' people; being male and female become more apparent to oneself with maturational changes

b) They are more attuned to forming relationships with peers; encourage enabling relationships especially with persons of their own gender

c) Your child requires mentorship on initiating, maintaining and terminating relationships constructively. You should also orient your child on healthy ways of handling peer pressure

Sharman, Cross, and Vennis (2004)

Your child might:
a) Need your experienced support as they deal with added
academic challenges. Your child naturally dislikes intrusion at this age, hence, you need to have a balanced approach in providing support where you allow your child to take the lead but you moderate

b) Show signs of wanting greater independence; he/she is now becoming differentiated though he/she maybe uncertain about his/her capacity to deal with his/ her life's challenges

c) Begin to attain capacity for empathy for others thus becoming a friendlier person to be with

d) Develop a bigger attention span and ability to process information more realistically

Safety and health measures for late Childhood Parenting

Safety Health

More independence and less adult supervision can put children at risk for injuries from falls and other accidents.

a) Help your child take care of him/ herself whenever he/she is riding in a vehicle. Motor vehicle crashes are the most common cause of death from unintentional injury among children of this age

b) Know where your child is and whether a responsible adult is present. Make plans with your child concerning when he/she will call you, where you can find him/her, and what time you expect him/her home etc

c) Make sure your child wears a helmet when riding a bike
d) Many children get home from school before their parents get home from work. It is important to have clear rules and plans for your child when he/she is home alone. Make sure you follow through with what you have set up so that your supervision is contained within defined
parameters
a) Provide a balanced diet with plenty of fruits and vegetables; limit foods high in solid fats, added sugars, or salt, and prepare healthier foods for family meals
b) Keep television sets out of your child's bedroom. Limit screen time, including computers and video games, to no more than 1 hour
c) Encourage your child to participate in an hour a day of physical activities that are age appropriate and enjoyable and
that offer variety. Make sure your child is doing three types of activities, aerobic (e.g. running), muscle strengthening
(e.g. climbing), and bone strengthening (e.g. jumping rope) at least three days per week

Sharman, Cross, and Vennis (2004) Kail (2011)

advice on late Childhood Parenting a. Help your child develop his/her own sense of right and wrong. Talk with him/her about risky things to engage in like smoking or dangerous physical drills and how to deal practically with peer pressure

b. Coach and mentor your child to have a clear sense of responsibility regarding personal hygiene, personal care, cleaning the environment, relationships, home chores, community social responsibility

c. Meet the families of your child's friends; get to know their values and their way of looking at life.This helps you appreciate the positives your children can be endowed with by interacting with those friends and communicate warning signals on lessons that would require rethinking or even discarding

d. Talk with your child about respecting others. Encourage him/ her to help people in need. Talk with him/her about what to do when others are not kind or are disrespectful

e. Spend time with your child. Talk with him/her about his/her friends, his/her accomplishments, and what challenges to expect. Children detest it when parents criticize their friends without any basis, they prefer balanced views

f. Be involved in your child's school. Attend school events; meet your child's teachers and administrators
g. Encourage your child to join school clubs such as a sports team, drama, environmental or to be a volunteer for a charity
h. Use discipline to guide and protect your child, instead of punishment to make him/her feel badly about himself
i. Encourage your child to develop healthy reading and study habits
j. Be affectionate and honest with your child, and do things together as a family. This builds family cohesion, oneness and a sense of belongingness
k. When using praise, help your child think about his/ her own accomplishments, by saying, "You must be proud of yourself" rather than "I'm proud of you." This encourages children from this early age to listen to their feelings and thoughts and make decisions about the direction they want to go
l. Help your child set his/her own goals. Encourage him/her to think about skills and abilities he/she would like to have and about how to develop them
m. Make clear rules and stick to them. Talk with your child about what you expect from him/her (behavior) among other siblings and in private so that he/she can feel respected. If you provide reasons for rules, it will help him/her know what to do in most situations
n. Talk with your child about the normal physical and emotional changes of puberty. If you ignore these lessons or delay to pre-empt experiences before they happen, your child can feel uncared for and his/her needs neglected.

Early adolescence (Teens) (12-14 years)

In this age bracket, your child has entered the early adolescent stage and hormonal changes are at an all-time high. This is a time of many physical, mental, emotional, and social changes. Most boys grow facial and pubic hair and their voices deepen while girls grow pubic hair and breasts, and start their periods. They might be worried about these changes and how they are viewed by others. Be on the lookout to find out whether your child is an early or late bloomer.

Children at this age are very sensitive about what might appear out of the normal and you should be there to resolve such fears. This also will be a time when your teen might face peer pressure to use alcohol, tobacco products, drugs and to have sex. Other challenges can be eating disorders, depression, and family problems. At this age, teens make more of their own choices about friends, sports, studying, and school. They become more independent with their own personality and interests, although parents are still very important.

Emotional and Social Development Thinking and Learning
Children in this age group might: Children in this age group might: a) Display keen interest on their looks and a) clothing

b) Fluctuate between high and low levels b) of confidence and self-reliance
c) Experience emotional highs and lows c) which may be very confusing for a
parent
d) Show keenness in relating with peers
and wanting to please them. Your child can attract lots of conflicts with you,
but that's not the way to go, you need
him/her more as a friend in order to
influence him/her positively
e) Feel a lot of sadness or depression,
which can lead to poor grades at
school, alcohol or drug use, unsafe sex, and other problems
f) Express less affection toward parents;
sometimes these children can be
arrogant and disrespectful
g) Feel stressed by challenging school
work
h) Develop eating problems due to high
levels of stress and anxiety or even
because of image issues
Have greater capacity for diverse thinking
Be better able to express feelings through talking Develop a stronger sense of right and wrong

Safety and health measures for Early adolescence Parenting
Safety Health
You play an important role in keeping your child safe, no matter how old he or she is. a) Make sure your teen follows regulations for safety like wearing seatbelts
b) Encourage your teen to wear

a helmet when riding a bike or protective garments when participating in any risky activities or sports

c) Talk with your teen about the dangers of drugs, drinking, smoking, and risky sexual activity. Ask him/ her what he/she knows and thinks about these issues, and share your thoughts and feelings with him/ her. Listen to what he/she says and answer his/her questions honestly and directly

d) Engage your teen about choice of friends who impart positively on his/ her life and ways of avoiding friends who have negative lifestyles. Let him/her know it's best to be his/her own person capable of directing his/ her life

e) Know where your teen is and whether a responsible adult is present. Make plans with him/her for when he/she will call you, where you can find him/her, and what time you expect him/her home

f) Set clear rules with your teen regarding who to relate deeply with, whom to take home, where to go and not go, TV and social media engagement, when to arrive home, how to treat elders and completing homework or household tasks

a) Inspire your teen to be
physically active through engaging in religious, social or sporting activities. Helping with household tasks such as cleaning dishes, washing clothes, cooking, fixing
broken items, cutting fodder for animals, feeding and grooming pets, trimming fences, polishing surfaces and removing cobwebs is a way he/she can make him/ herself useful while energizing oneself

b) Meal time is very important for families. Eating together helps teens make better choices about the foods they eat, promotes healthy weight, and gives your family members time to talk with each other

c) Limit screen time for your child to not more than 1 to 2 hours per day of quality programming, at home, school, or afterschool care

Kail (2011)

advice for Early adolescent Parenting
a. Update your knowledge on drugs, sex and technology so that you can explore with your teen the pros and cons. You also need to use your experience to guide your child on these vital areas

b. When there is a conflict,be clear about goals and expectations (like getting good grades, keeping things clean, and showing respect), but allow your teen's input on how to reach those goals (like when and how to study or clean)

c. Meet and get to know your teen's friends and acquaintances d. Show an interest in your teen's school and social life e. Help your teen make healthy decisions and choices that are in

line with his/her life's goals
f. Respect your teen's opinions and take into account his/her thoughts and feelings. It is important that he/she knows you

are listening to him/her

middle adolescence (15-18 years)

In the Kenyan context, children in this age group are between form one and four. This period is both exciting and challenging for you and your teen. Emotions can change quickly as your teen learns to deal with school, friends, personal evaluation and adult expectations. Your teen's self-esteem is affected by success in school, sports, and friendships. During this time, your teen may naturally compare him/herself with others and he/she might form false ideas about his/her body image. You should patiently listen so that you can correct these false beliefs in time before they affect other aspects of life. The influence of TV, magazines, and the Internet can add to your teen's poor body image.

Harding (2013) believes that most girls will be physically mature by now, and most will have completed puberty. Boys are also maturing physically during this time. Your teen might have concerns about her body size,shape,or weight.Eating disorders are also common,especially among girls. During this time, your teen is developing his/her unique personality and opinions. Relationships with friends are still important, yet your teen will have other interests as he/she develops a more clear sense of who he/she is. This is also an important time to prepare for more independence and responsibility; many teenagers are finalizing their high school.

Sharman, Cross, and Vennis (2004) outlines some emotional, social and mental aspects for children at this stage:

Emotional and Social Development Thinking and Learning

Your teen might: Your teen might: a) Start showing more interest a) in the opposite sex, this is perfectly in order and it b) is now your role to teach on healthy and unhealthy opposite sex relationships c)

b) Exhibit more independence from you which is part of growing up

c) Reveal deeper capacity for caring and loving others and for developing more intimate relationships

d) Show desire to spend more
time with friends than you
or other family members

e) Feel a lot of sadness or
depression, which can lead
to poor grades at school,
alcohol or drug use, unsafe
sex, and other problems

Carry out more defined tasks and chores in more thorough ways
Shows more concern on relationship between his/her studies and future career
Be better at rationalizing their
decisions and choices and their values and beliefs are more clearly defined

Safety and health measures for middle adolescence Parenting

Safety a) Engage your teenage child on dangers of reckless driving on the road. Their excitement makes them oblivious of dangers of such escapades

b) Their perspective of death is limited and unrealistic. David Elkind (1967) uses the term adolescent egocentrism to describe adolescents' inability to distinguish between their perception of what others think about them and what people actually think in reality. According to Elkind, adolescent egocentrism results in two consequential mental constructions, namely imaginary audience and personal fable Imaginary audience is a term that Elkind uses to describe the phenomenon that an adolescent anticipates the reactions of other people to him/herself in actual or impending social situations. Elkind argues that this kind of anticipation could be explained by the adolescent's preoccupation that others are as admiring or as critical of him as he is of himself. As a result, an audience is created, as the adolescent believes that he/she will be the focus of attention, some people criticizing and others admiring him/her
Personal Fable is the term Elkind created to describe this notion, which is the complement of the construction of imaginary audience. Since an adolescent usually fails to differentiate his focus on his own perceptions and that of others, he tends to believe that he is of importance to so many people (the imaginary audiences) that he comes to regard his feelings as something special and unique. This belief in personal uniqueness and invincibility becomes an illusion that he can be above some of the rules, disciplines and laws that apply to other people; even consequences such as death (Frankenberger, 2000)
Due to the existence of personal fable at some point, an adolescent tends to substitute the roles of an idol, a hero or even God with his/her own image. That explains why they can participate in hazardous undertakings which are obviously risky in other people's judgment. Hence he/she can engage in risky behaviors like sex and drugs.

Health a) Encourage your teen to get enough sleep and physical activity, and to eat healthy, balanced meals. Make sure your teen gets 1 hour or more of physical activity each day

b) Encourage your teen to have meals with the family. Eating together will help your teen make better choices about the foods he/she eats, promote healthy weight, and give family members time to talk with each other. In addition, a teen who eats meals with the family is more likely to get better grades and less likely to smoke, drink, or use drugs, and also less likely to get into fights, think about suicide, or engage in sexual activity
Kail (2011)

Salgaa Road Accident
On New Year's Eve 2015, four teenagers were killed in a road accident while three others survived at a black spot in Salgaa, Nakuru County, Kenya. It was reported that the teenager who was driving did not have a driver's license.The owner of the vehicle,a police officer said he had given the vehicle to a friend only to learn that the following day it was involved in an accident. It was reported that parents of the deceased were shocked to learn of the incident, as they knew the teenagers had gone to church to celebrate the New Year.

Teenagers Behaving Badly
The Daily Nation on Thursday, August 6th 2015 reported an incident where 45 students from various secondary schools were arrested and locked up at Kiangwachi Police Patrol Base in Kirinyaga County, Kenya after some of them were found in possession of bhang, tobacco and engaging in a sexual orgy inside a Nairobi bound bus. "This was a proper city nganya, a pimped-up matatu, complete with a deafening exhaust, blaring music, garish spray-painted graffiti and saucy inscriptions such as,'Babie while you were away….I became a millionaire" and "Why go to high school when you can't go to school high," the story read. Residents of Kibirigwi and Kiangwachi on the Karatina-Nairobi road in Nyeri could not believe it when they saw what the girls and boys, still in their school uniforms, were doing through the windows of the matatu.

In another incident, it was reported in the local media that in Eldoret, 500 students were arrested for engaging in intoxication and sex in a nightclub. It was reported that some of the students were found in possession of bhang and used condoms.

These incidents validate the claim that adolescents can easily be excitable without thinking about consequences of their actions. Did they think about the legal and disastrous consequences of being driven by another teenager without a driver's license? Were they concerned about being crowded in a small vehicle? Had they thought what would happen if the owner of the vehicle saw them driving his vehicle without his approval? Was enjoyment and adventure much more important than their safety and wellbeing? Trying to find answers to these questions brings out one reality; that teenagers can have gross miscalculations sometimes to their detriment.

The incidents demonstrate the extent adolescents go in search of gratification and enjoyment. It would seem they do not think much about the effect of their behaviors to themselves and others. An element of peer pressure is evident in the incidents and therefore their inability to be self-driven.

As a parent then, you have to help your adolescent child to define him/herself to be able to self-regulate and provide him/herself selfdirection and self-respect. Talk with your teen about suicide and pay attention to warning signs. Talk with your teen about the dangers of drugs, drinking, smoking, and risky sexual activity. Ask him/her what he knows and thinks about these issues, and share your feelings and thoughts with him/her. Listen to what he/she says and answer his/her questions honestly and directly.

advice on middle adolescence Parenting
a. Encourage your teen to develop friendships that add value to him/her

b. Encourage your teen to volunteer in activities in school and within the community
c. Compliment your teen and celebrate his/her efforts and accomplishments
d. Let your teen know you love and celebrate him/her through your conversations and actions
e. Help your teen develop logical thinking patterns through critically evaluating the pros and cons of his/her decisions
f. Let your teen know you have the capacity to listen to his/her pains, hurts, struggles, achievements and joys. Children this age easily develop depressive moods and you should be on the lookout so that you can help him/her process these emotions before they become problematic
g. Help your teen become skillful in problem solving. You can create scenarios like peer pressure, sexual promiscuity, drug abuse or criminality. Help your teen to think sensibly how he/ she would deal with these challenges
h. Your teen will naturally crave for privacy, respect this need and instead be open to his/her struggles and needs without being judgmental
i. You will enhance your teen in academic, relational and vocational capacities when you support his/her school and extracurricular activities in and out of school. You help him/her achieve all round growth

j. Your teen can easily get addicted to social media, watching TV and browsing the Internet, motivate him/her to make decisions regarding how those activities can be made useful

late adolescence (19-23 years)

Gilbert and I are parenting Kenna and Keega in their late adolescence, 19 and 20 years. In the beginning, it was very chaotic because we were tightening the rules and they were becoming outraged. One time, our children warned us that we would lose them if we continued being high handed. Undeniably, they were hurting and it was evident in their expression. They could not understand why we were restricting their use of the family vehicle, while we gave our workers a free hand to use it. "Are your workers more of your children than we are; you seem to trust them more than you trust us," they retorted.This statement coming from our children was an awakening for us. From our observation, they were very impulsive while driving and we reckoned they needed more experience under supervision but they could not see it that way. We decided we would make a bargain with them, through making rules, which were going to take care of everyone in the family and protect them from any harm.

Late adolescence is a period when youngsters are transitioning to adulthood. In Kenya, they are joining college or the university and they are starting a life of their own. They want to live by their own rules but they also expect their parents to accommodate them. At this time, you may experience him/her as headstrong and not wanting to adhere to your standards. This can make you feel scared of what would happen to him/her. Nonetheless, he/she would want to be trusted by you, and this is the only wayyou will have positive influence on him/her.In addition, the late adolescents are serious about opposite sex relationships and it is easy to have unplanned pregnancy. Others engage in drugs, pornography and illicit affairs. However, they are unsure of themselves because they are grounding themselves. Sometimes, they are rather erratic in their responses to situations they are going through.

Emotional and Social Development Thinking and Learning

Youngsters in this age group might: Youngsters in this age group might: a) Indulge in alcohol and drug abuse a) Have faulty thinking. Your in ways that affect their lifestyle and youngster can be disturbed performance in school. You have to with his/her body image help your youth to refrain from such though he/she may not risky behaviors have a visible problem.

b) Involve themselves in irresponsible Some concerns your sexual encounters that can youth may have include predispose them to sexually a big body, big tummy, transmitted infections flat buttocks, baldhead,

c) Relate more intimately with friends big breasts, tallness and and associations outside family. They smallness. Do not explain are on their way out of the family away whatever concern

d) Get discouraged and depressed due your young adult may have; to unmet expectations. For example, be ready to listen and help if a romantic relationship is terminated him/her accept him/herself prematurely, a youth easily becomes more
depressed owing to a deep sense of b) Can be wildly compulsive rejection and erratic in their actions.

e) Become suicidal due to feelings of The risky behaviors they failure, helplessness, uselessness exude like drinking and and hopelessness irresponsible sexual

engagements are an indicator of this c) Can feel more than they

think through situations; this explains their prevalent depressive moods

Safety and health measures for late adolescent Parenting
Safety Health

a) Talk with your young adult about the dangers of drugs, drinking, smoking, and risky sexual activity. Ask him/her what he/ she knows and thinks about these issues, and share your thoughts and feelings with him/ her. Listen to what he/she says and answer his/her questions honestly and directly. Look around you; you may remember a child of a friend who went to college/university and started abusing drugs and engaging in risky sexual activity. Finishing schooling could also have been difficult

b) Remind your young adult about the dangers of being caught with illegal drugs like marijuana, heroin and cocaine

c) Remind your young adult about the dangers of having risky sexual behaviors and the aftermath of that: infections, abortions, infertility and
depressive episodes

d) Make sure your young adult has learnt all the rudiments of safe driving before you give him/ her full mandate to drive on his/ her own

a) Young people engage in health-risk behaviors like consumption of alcohol, marijuana and other hard drugs. You have to discuss with your young adult adverse consequences on health associated with use and abuse of drugs

b) Young people have a high susceptibility of contracting sexually transmitted diseases due to their permissive lifestyles and unsafe sexual adventures. Help your young adult appreciate the health concerns related to irresponsible sexual engagements

c) Young people are predisposed to mental health problems like panic attacks, anxiety, depressions, suicidal tendencies due to shifting self-esteem and inability to honestly examine situations. Let your young adult know you will be there for him/her when processing hurtful and painful experiences

d) Young people engage in risky driving behaviors either by driving at high speed due to adrenalin rush or driving under the influence of alcohol and drugs. I find our 19 year old having the tendency to race against other vehicles when driving and having a need to be seen as a hero. In his mind, he is unmindful of danger that lurks ahead. We want him to become conscious of this fact by putting him in a supervised program until he masters self-regulation. Help your youngster take responsibility of their life through responsible driving

e) Young women are too conscious of their weight and as a result, they may eat much less than their bodies requires. They are looking after their body image in this way without thinking about how unhealthy it really is. Encourage your young adult to eat healthy and to be realistic about body image. They can also over exercise with the intent of cutting down their weight even when they don't have a weight problem

Sally's & Dally's Case
Sally and Dally are parents of an 18-year-old boy and a 14-year-old girl. Their son's 18th birthday was two days ago, and he is now pressuring them to let him do whatever he wants. Example: stay out at night until 12:00 or maybe later. He says they are not treating him like an adult. The parents keep reminding him that he still has five months of school left, and soon he will be off to college, where he will be making his own set of rules for himself. They want to keep a good relationship with him, but they sometimes do not know the right words to use.

Certainly, Sally and Dally are feeling frustrated and strained. They appreciate their son is growing to be an adult, but he is asking for autonomy without even earning it. It's usual to have a difficult time with a growing adolescent, but parents have to contend with the reality that the child still requires guidance to make realistic decisions and choices. He/she is still inexperienced and he/she can put him/herself in risky situations through absolute freedom. Hence, you should allow yourself to have collaborative engagements with your young adults so that you can help them make constructive decisions.

advice on late adolescent Parenting
a. You should collaborate with your young adult in setting rules, which protect him/her from harm and contribute to family cohesiveness. For example, No verbal insults are allowed, no drugs and alcohol, no lying etc. Those rules should be very clear because you don't want to start having double standards with older children, especially if you have other younger children in the home

b. If you feel compromised and taken advantage of by an older child, you need to realize this; the child is an adult now. Let your adolescent child know you appreciate this fact but also that he/she is living under your roof

c. You have to let go of some life ownership you felt towards your child. *"We are responsible for you in regulating your actions,"* should change to *"We accept that you make your own decisions and that you must deal with the consequences."*

d. You have to let go of some strict controls you had on your adolescent child, *"You must conduct yourself as a member of this family,"* should change to *"We accept that you must become your own person, and take charge of your life."*

e. You have to let go of some life agenda you had for the child, *"We determine the direction you take,"* should change to *"We accept that you must set your own course through life."*

f. You have to help your young adult manage his/her disappointments, failures, losses and unmet expectations. He/ she needs you to be there for him/her for reassurance

g. Hold risk reduction talks on issues like radicalization, drug abuse, sexual lifestyle and compulsivity in carrying out tasks like driving or cycling and mental health conditions (anxiety, panic, depression and suicidal ideations) related to their life's experiences

h. Help your youth define qualities he/she would consider in a spouse and values and beliefs related to healthy relationships and marriages. Exploring this subject can empower your young adult to make informed choices and decisions

i. Help your young adult accept his/her body image through giving positive feedback and rationally discussing concerns he/ she may have without explaining them away. Equally, help him/ her deal with emerging fears of the unknown

j. Let your young adult know he/she needs to prepare adequately to face the real world. Help him/her to identify ways of grounding him/herself
Parentng Styles and Role Modelling

Chapter 4

ChaPTEr fOur
ParENTNg STylES aNd rOlE mOdElliNg

There are only two lasting endowments we can hope to bequeath our children. One of these is roots, the other, wings. **Johann wolfgang von goethe**

In everything you do as a person, you have a particular preference. As a parent then, there is a particular method or style you use in raising your child, a method that is natural to you. For instance, you may be that parent who gives your child liberty to do what he/she wants, or you may be that parent who likes to know whatever the child is doing at any time. Most times the styles that parents use are not well thought out and are largely informed by the kind of parenting they received when they were young.As a parent,I find myself parenting my children the way my mother parented us which is already automated within me. I use my training in counselling to moderate and enhance my parenting orientation and the activities therein.

Your parenting style is the outfit that informs your input in rearing your child. The parenting style they choose should therefore be clear to you so that you can evaluate its impact. Your parenting style as Johann Wolfgang von Goethe said should give your children roots (foundation) and wings (ability to have multi-dimensional success). Hence, parenting should never be practiced from guesswork but should be evidence based; meaning it must reliably be proven to work. Apostle Paul warns in Colossians 3: 12 (NIV), *"Fathers, do not embitter your children, or they will become discouraged."* This scripture urges fathers to be sensitive and considerate in dealing with their children so that they (the children) can experience motivation and therefore go about life with confidence. Proper parenting is mindful of input, aware that the input determines output, that is, the kind of people you eventually release to the society.

Parenting Styles
You somehow know you use a certain method to parent your child

though you may not have given it a name or much thought. When you compare your parenting style with that of your spouse or friend, you can cite some glaring differences. This means every parent uses his/her own personalized style to parent, informed by experiences and knowledge acquired. Baumrind (1966) came up with three general parenting styles: authoritative, authoritarian, and permissive while Maccoby, and Martin (1983) expanded these styles to four, namely authoritative, authoritarian, indulgent and neglectful. All these styles are in a continuum of aloofness and irresponsibility and being controlling and demanding. These styles of parenting feature combinations of acceptance and responsiveness on the one hand and demand and control on the other.

There is immense lack of awareness regarding styles parents use and how they influence child development. As parents, we must parent consciously, being careful of our input in developing wellrounded children. In my counselling with parents, I often hear parents quarrelling and arguing over the particular styles their partners are using. Each parent feels and fears the other parent is not careful enough in parenting and the style he/she uses is inadequate to shape their children.

Dida and Kinga's Case
Dida is apprehensive over the style of parenting her husband Kinga uses. He too does not trust her method. He believes in talking with their two male children when they commit a felony, while she believes in "spare the rod and spoil the child." He too is anxious when she takes the belt and rushes outside to whip the children. He holds her hand firmly and stops her in her tracks. This makes Dida withdraw and she does not talk for days on end. She brushes off his method of parenting and believes he is just too ineffective with the children. Her husband also believes she is too ruthless with the children and does not apply helpful corrective measures. He says in desperation, "they are children, allow them to make mistakes and correct them realistically."

Both Dida and Kinga do not agree on supportive methods of parenting their children. They, like other parents argue endlessly and do not reach an agreement. Both their parenting approaches are okay but they should be modified to be responsive to particular issues, situations, needs and developmental stages.

authoritative Parenting (Just right)

Authoritative parenting can be referred to as balanced, situational parenting.

As a parent, you respond according to the dictates of the situation requiring your rejoinder or input. Baumrind explains that an authoritative parent is both demanding and responsive. Authoritative parenting, also called balanced parenting, is characterized by a child-centered approach that demands high expectation of maturity, compliance to parental rules and direction while allowing for open dialogue between the parent and child concerning those rules and behaviors.

If you are an authoritative parent, you are able to identify the capacities you want to grow in your children and evaluate levels of achievement of those competences. You work with your child to identify abilities required; tasks that will help achieve them and ways of measuring success rates. Such abilities would be physical in nature like cleaning clothes, cooking and wiping surfaces. Emotional competences would entail management of emotions like anger, resentment and hurt. You are keen on identifying abilities your child requires at each developmental stage. You are a friend and a coach to your child. You help your child identify and respect limits. For example, if he/she is angered by a friend, he/she should not beat or insult that friend because it is abusive. You punish wrongdoing but you agree on dos, don'ts, and ways of rewarding good and bad behavior. Your expectations from your children are clearly stipulated and you allow your children to clarify what they do not understand. The eventual parenting product you desire is a mature, self-driven, self-regulating, and others-respecting, integrated individual.

Baumrind says authoritative parents are not usually controlling; they allow children reasonable freedom to explore so that they can make their own decisions, based upon their own reasoning. This is the most recommended style of parenting by child-rearing experts. You should aim at being an authoritative parent who is available for your child but also providing him/her space to adventure and develop self.

Cynthia's Case
On her wedding day, Cynthia, 25 years old, woke up feeling tearful. She was about to leave home to get married to the love of her life. She came from a humble background compared to her friends' families, but she had a lot of appreciation for her parents. Cynthia's parents had arranged to have a brief

prayer session with their daughter before she prepared for her great day. Cynthia started by thanking her parents for being loving, firm, supervising her tasks, monitoring her progress, explaining reasons for their punishment, encouraging her to participate in religious activities and trusting her to be responsible in all situations. She remembered from the age of 12 years that she and her siblings were involved in setting rules, regulations and limits that were to regulate their conduct. Most of her peers admired her for her balanced maturity and looked up to her as a mentor. She said to her parents, "Mum and Dad, thank you for modeling me to be outstanding; I will be a capable wife and mother of my children."

Cynthia is profoundlyappreciative of the informed sacrificial efforts her parents had put in bringing her up and feels those lessons will make her a good wife and mother in her next stage of life. Their structured parenting style aided Cynthia in having clarity about how to deal with different aspects of life, marriage and family included.

authoritarian Parenting (Too rigid)
This style of parenting is largely controlling of the child while you expect total obedience. Baumrind explains that as an authoritarian parent, you aim to shape, control, and evaluate the behavior and attitudes of the child in accordance with a set standard of conduct, usually an absolute standard. Authoritarian parents believe they have no business listening to the sentiments of their children. They believe they know what is best for their children and they should not be questioned. Such parents 'know it all' and they feel children should be seen and not heard.

As an authoritarian parent, you obviously love order, structure and decorum at the expense of molding your children to be unique and self-driven. You are denying your child the ability to think for him/ herself, tackle his/her own challenges and develop creativity in his/her approach to situations. Such children experience emptiness, 'lostness' and lack of confidence in dealing with life's situations because their parents have always been their drivers and they resigned to the passenger's place. When an authoritarian parent decides to discipline his/her child, he/she does not bother to discuss the expectations and consequences of not following through with set rules and standards.

Phillipe's Case

Phillipe, a form two student, is brought up by a father who believes in strict regulations. Phillipe's father does not understand what makes it difficult for anyone to follow laid-down rules. Lately, Phillipe has started having discipline problems in school. He has been writing open notes, which have been given to his parents. In those notes, he threatens to commit suicide and he is very aggressive in his relationships with others around him. His father does not understand where this behavior originated from since he has set clear rules and regulations for Phillipe. As a result, the school counsellor has advised the father to practice flexibilityon the son because he is now an adolescent who is discovering himself and naturally requires space to find himself.

Phillipe's story clarifies that being high handed and controlling makes children fragile, purposeless and empty. Such children like Phillipe are not able to develop internal strongholds of self-acceptance, selfconfidence, self-efficacy, clarity of thinking, resilience, self-ambition and self-direction because they are always directed by others. Children should be allowed to be their own chauffeurs rather than being driven by others.

Permissive/indulgent Parenting
Being permissive literally means routinely or habitually accommodating or being tolerant of habits or behaviors that others might frown at or forbid. According to Baumrind, these parents do not make tough demands on the children but they highly respond to their needs. This parenting style is characterized by low demandingness with high responsiveness. Children reared by such parents assume that other people owe them and should always fix their needs. They are highly undisciplined and lack a sense of limits because their parents hardly regulate their wishes, desires and actions. They are not taught to be responsible hence they are not responsive to situations. They view other people as reservoirs to draw from, hence they dehumanize other people.

They do not develop a perspective of dealing effectively with a real world that expects individuals to be evaluative, calculative and responsive to ongoing situations. As a permissive parent, you are overly responsive to your child's demands, seldom enforcing consistent rules. Later in life, your children are unable to adhere to rules, regulations and externally defined standards. They make other people feel frustrated because they are not sensitive and responsive to them. They make poor friends, colleagues, workers, spouses and family members because they are grossly selfish, manipulative and incapable of meeting other people's needs. They are the spoilt brats of the world, and they face terrible rejection from the world that in turn makes them miserable.

Pepe's Case
Pepe's wife complains that her husband is controlled by his mother. Pepe is an only child of a single mother who was very possessive of him. His mother used to do everything for him even when he was a big boy. She did not train him to be available for other people. He learnt that other people have to attend to him but not vice versa. Other women used to remark that Pepe will never make a good husband because he was too selfish. Now as an adult, Pepe lives this script and does not understand why his wife complains about it. He did not re-define his relationship with his doting mother when he got married. Pepe resents hearing this worn out story from his wife and tells her as much. He recently separated from his wife who vowed never to reunite with him again and Pepe has gone back to stay with his mother, saying that, that has always been his place.

Children of permissive/indulgent parents like Pepe are clueless regarding other people's needs. They lack personal discipline that was not instilled in them and their sense of right and wrong is not in tune with reality. Pepe does not seem to appreciate how he should treat his wife so that they can both be happy. Such children become co-dependents (unhealthily relying on others and letting others rely on them for survival) throughout life. Does Pepe have a life beyond the mother? He needs to craft his own destiny which will give him joy, happiness and contentment. His mother too should help Pepe cut the harmful attachment with her so that healthier, more realistic relationships can be formed. Pepe too needs to develop sensitivity and develop healthy boundaries with other people.

Neglectful Parenting
Maccoboy, and Martin (1983) observe that neglectful parenting is neither demanding nor responsive. Neglectful parenting is also called uninvolved, detached, dismissive or hands-off parenting. As a parent, you can be

neglectful through not physically or emotionally being there for your child. You may also expect your child to carry out roles he/she is not developmentally capable of doing or you may not have coached your child to carry out the task. You may also not be emotionally attached to your child,thus lacking sufficient bonding.You may not have prepared your child adequately for future age-related experiences like handling oneself when going through menstrual periods. This can make your daughter feel denied, not respected and lost since she doesn't know how to respond to this emerging need. A child who is trained feels accomplished, in control and self-reliant in handling issues.

Phoebe's Case

Phoebe's parents are high-flying, career parents with demanding jobs. They are sometimes sent out of the country on official duties and Phoebe and her siblings are left with an aunt who is very dismissive and has her fair share of emotional problems. The children feel their aunt and even their parents are unavailable for them. Phoebe has been engaging in heavy masturbation and is already addicted to pornography. She tells her friend that she does this to deal with her emptiness and feelings of being lost. She admires children of not-well-to-do families because their parents are always available for them. Teachers describe Phoebe as a very glamorous but hollow girl who lacks focus in things that matter most.

Phoebe's parents are perfect providers of material needs but her emotional, relational, spiritual and cognitive needs are hardly met. Certainly, Phoebe will always be an inadequate, unfocused and irresponsible adult due to neglectful, ignorant parenting. Phoebe's parents have to sacrifice their careers; possibly pick careers that will make them more available to their children. Phoebe just needs them for a few years and she will be ready for take-off. They can at that juncture pick up their career ambitions single mindedly.

role modeling for Children

Children naturally learn through imitation and replication. You and other significant persons to the child are the perfect models. Children watch what others do and they duplicate that. What they imitate can be either positive or negative. This includes dressing, talking, resolving issues, dealing with emotions, cooking and cleaning. You would want to model positive beliefs, values and attitudes. Adults in the 21st century are rather careless regarding behaviors and experiences they expose to young children.

Nowadays, children are constantly tuned to television, radio, smart phones and the internet watching and listening to diverse issues or images some of which are not age appropriate. The FM stations feature talk shows about criminality, romance and sex. Some of these programs are poisonous to the mind and they rob children of their innocence before they are of age to understand such adult issues. Many children today glamorize media personalities to the extent of wanting to be like them. You need to limit the amount of time your children spend watching television, browsing the internet and being on social media. You are placed in the best position to model a positive lifestyle and appropriate capabilities to your child. You should be very intentional about what you role model for your children. Qualities that you can role model include honesty, integrity, compassion, fortitude, dependability, high standards and values.

Qualities of a Positive role model

Self and Others' respect
Your child will learn most from you through observation. He/she picks the way you carry yourself and he/she will model that. You display selfrespect if you eat well, dress well, focus on life tasks, have personalized plans on your activities and you engage in activities that attend to your self-care. Equally, you are sensitive to other people and you are available for them but you also create helpful boundaries in those relationships.

model responsibility
You display multi-faceted responsibility, you take responsibility of what you do, feel and think, and you are aware of possible consequences. You only promise what you are certain you will carry through to the end and you are consistent with processes. That way, your child will learn to take responsibility and to deliver his/her promises.

Be well rounded
Your child is definitely watching you to learn how he/she can ensure well roundedness. He/she should observe you in action allotting your time to

attend to your physical wellbeing, health, emotional wellbeing, spirituality, social life, vocation, recreation and intellectual pursuits. He/ she also realizes that life is multi-dimensional and everything in life matters. If your child sees you exercising regularly, he/she internalizes that physical wellbeing is an important aspect of life.

rational decision and Choice making
Let your child know that decision and choice making should be informed by facts and knowledge. He/she needs to appreciate that decisions and choices ought to be well thought out so that consequences are factored. Think out aloud when you are dealing with situations that require solutions or choices, that way, your child is able to pick some principles that matter most in the decision and choice making process. For example, you may be dealing with a quarrelsome neighbor. You may say aloud, *"I do not want to engage in quarrels with baba Steve because I will end up burdening myself with unnecessary anger and stress. I will also make my children hate him and yet if anything happens to us, he would be the first to call upon for assistance. Whenever he starts picking issues that can result to quarrels, I will respond with respect and thoughtfulness."*

Self-discipline
Discipline begets success in life. You want your child to be successful in all facets of life. For this to happen, your child must develop self-control and self-regulation. This means he/she can willingly gravitate towards helpful actions and refrain at will from harmful experiences. This way, he/she will achieve unprecedented outputs in life. Your child will learn to exercise willpower, resolve and strength of character because he/ she has seen it modeled.

honesty
Your child should learn the essence of being honest with self, other people and situations. Help him/her experience the liberty and peace that comes with being honest. Your child will start realizing, being truthful makes one vulnerable; an okay experience amongst humankind.

The Case of Maurice
Maurice, a father of two had a child outside wedlock. His wife knew about this but they were not sure it was okay to tell the children. However, they

figured, someone might tell them one day or they get wind of it from unlikely quarters. So, they decided they were the ones to tell them. When they did, the children were heart-broken and they cried bitterly. At that instant, they felt betrayed by their dad whom they held in high regard. Nonetheless, when they were through, the younger child looked straight at his dad and said, "Dad, thanks for allowing yourself to be vulnerable to tell us this. We now realize how deep your love is for us, you have braced shame so that you can shield us from pain and anguish in future. You have made us value truthfulness and openness in life." Maurice could not help but shed tears of appreciation and serenity. He turned to his wife and muttered, "Thank you darling for daring to walk with me through this. I wouldn't have managed alone."

integrity

All children have a belief that their parents are ideal and beyond reproach. This explains why children get crushed when they come to know about the dark side of their parents. Your child expects you to be a good example in conduct and in speech. He/she will naturally get disappointed when you turn out to be the exact opposite. Your child expects you to shun indulging in gossip, using drugs and alcohol or even refraining from extra marital affairs. They have no power to make you stop the shaming, destructive behaviors but they hurt and become shame-faced. By doing this, you set your child to also follow suit to his/her detriment. Wouldn't you redefine yourself for the sake of your beloved child?

Coach on Processes

Your child needs to understand how some situations build up and how they can be detonated. For example, he/she needs to understand how anger manifests itself and how it can be resolved. He/she should know he/she gets angry because situations or certain persons are perceived to be unfair to him/her or he/she is letting him/herself down and therefore he/she is angry with self or at other times, God is unfair or ruthless in certain situations. Pinpointing helps clarify the source of anger. Help your child challenge unrealistic thoughts and perceptions. Then, he/she can identify options in resolution of anger. When this process is repeated many times, it becomes a lifestyle. Your role is one of coaching your child to appreciate the relief that comes from moving through a logical process.

apologize and admit mistakes

Children should be made to appreciate that nobody is perfect. When you make a bad choice, let your child know that you made a mistake and demonstrate how you correct it. By apologizing, admitting your mistake, and repairing the damage, you will be demonstrating an important yet an often-overlooked part of being a role model. This will help them understand that everyone makes mistakes and making mistakes is not the end of the world; you can correct a wrong to attain helpful results; and you should take responsibility for it as soon as possible.

Quality Time in Parenting

Quality time is time spent with a child where there is a true connection between the parent and child. In many cases, it may mean undivided attention. Deuteronomy 11:19 says, *"Teach them to your children, talking about them when you sit at home and when you walk along the road, when you lie down and when you get up."* This means you should be a wellorganized, devoted teacher and friend who knows the vital lessons to be taught to your children. Have you taught them about sensitivity and respect of others? What about work ethics? Have you forgotten lessons on modesty and good grooming? What about personal integrity and dignity? At the very least, for it to be quality time, your child needs to feel connected with you. If mom is reading while the child plays on the floor, it is quality time if when the child calls for mom's attention to something he or she is doing, and mom responds and interacts. However, it is not quality time if mom responds to the child with "not now, I am reading."

meticulously weave it all in

Your self-care,career,education pursuit,businesses,social engagements, religious activities, political ambitions, marriage and your parenting obligation have to be patterned seamlessly like a jigsaw puzzle. You as a parent have a myriad of activities to attend to on a daily basis but you should be a good planner so that activities do not become more important than your child. Quality time entails:

a. Setting time apart to be with your child away from distractions b. Creating a conducive environment for your child to open up c. Sharing fun and laughter with your child

d. Providing age appropriate guidance

e. Coaching your child on relevant abilities

f. Celebrating your child over achievements and accomplishments g. Organizing visits to friends and other appropriate social

gatherings for exposure

h. Carrying out mutual tasks

It is possible to give the wrong message in the name of quality time. If you always drop whatever you are doing to respond to a child, you may give the child a warped sense of importance. If there are no boundaries about when a child can or cannot interrupt, to the point where he or she develops an attitude that he or she can interrupt at any time or in any place, the message that is received is that the child is the most important person in the world. Such a child expects the whole world to stop so that his or her needs are met because that is what they have learnt.

Balancing work and Quality Time with Children

Work demands can come in the way of you being adequately available for your child. You may be employed or you may be an entrepreneur but such demands can be overwhelming in a world where you have to work with defined targets and performance contracts. You may notice you are carrying work home and you are not able to attend to your child the way you would love to. Sometimes you may be required to attend seminars, conferences or work assignments away from home. You may feel guilty because your children maybe communicating they feel deserted and uncared for. You must strive to achieve a work vs. quality time balance; otherwise, you will lose your children.

Penina's Case

Penina, a career banker is not happy at age 58. She has risen up the ladder in her career growth faster than any of her friends. However, she recalls it has come at a huge cost. Three of her adult children are heroin addicts while one ran away from home and she hardly visits. She says she did not have time for her children during their puberty and adolescent years. They are complete strangers to her. She feels she exchanged the well-being of her children with career advancement and money. She is being treated for depression and she admits it has resulted from shame, pain and anguish of seeing her children who passed through national schools go down the drain. These were indeed misplaced priorities and she will have to contend with a very bitter and worrisome old age.

Penina's case is not isolated, it happens all the time. She was oblivious of the impact of her misplaced priorities. She cannot rectify the mishap now because the children are now grown up. She has to live with the consequences of her omissions, which seem horrid.

Self-actualization and Quality Time with Children

We are living in a fast-paced world where it is easy for parenting to be pushed to the rear as parents chase their daily pursuits. In the 20th century, having a stable, cohesive family was a dream cherished by many. With modernism, globalization, industrialization and outflow of people to towns and abroad, there has been a value shift in what contributes to success in life. In Kenya, travelling abroad is viewed as progressive and many people hunger for that opportunity. Because of this trend, many children have been left with relatives or friends as parents seek greener pastures. Such children experience abandonment and disfranchisement when their parents leave. The damage meted on the children sometimes is not repairable. Think about this, as a parent, you will only have to sacrifice for 23 years to get your child all set for launching. The sacrifice is worth it and it indemnifies your child from harm inflicted by neglect.As you actualize,and as you look for the feelgood experiences, know that your child may suffer emptiness, rejection and lack of consistent support.

Santana's Case

Santana has been struggling with drugs and indiscipline in school. She has extreme arrogance and disrespect towards adults. She says adults are insensitive to children's needs. She has been brought up by her grandparents for the last twelve years. She is provided for with everything luxurious she wants but she confesses she is not happy because she feels those things are intended to blind her from the reality of being deserted. She longs for time with her mother, which is hard to come by. She tells her friends she can do anything to bring her mother back. She feels lonely and dejected.

The case of Santana decries the folly of pursuing wealth and feel-good experiences at the expense of your child. She does not feel important and that is the reason she indulges in drugs, indiscipline and high-level insensitivity. Since she has not experienced love and care, she has no idea how she would express the same to others.

Suggestions on Enjoying Quality Time with your Children You will have to calculatedly plan for quality time with you child. If you do not, other responsibilities in this exceedingly demanding world will take center stage. Giving quality time to your child will without doubt communicate to your child that he/she comes first before anything else. It makes him/her feel cherished and significant in life.Your child learns to hold him/herself in high esteem and does not allow other people to demean him/her. Providing quality time to your child is an act of love, which is very much treasured by your child. Planning well helps you strike a good balance on quantity and quality time required by your child. Your child is not interested in quantity of time but quality time.

a) Plan for fun activities with your child

Identify activities and tasks that can mutually give you enjoyment and laughter. This may include visits, recreation activities, participating in talent shows, carrying out home chores together and watching sports. This creates bonding and opportunities to know each other. You will embed in your child a happy personality that goes easy with situations.

b) isolate time dedicated to your child

In the midst of your tight schedules, set aside time to be with your child. This time can be planned for so that other activities do not get in the way. Your child will appreciate the determination you have in getting mutual time to be together. This will make your child develop a stable sense of confidence and self-acceptance.

c) Plan for mutual activities

If you want to undertake activities together, identify those that both of you delight in. Involving your child in choosing those activities ingrains sureness in your child. He/she starts developing a sense of worth and self-belief, which catapults him/her to successes in life's exploits. **d) Create boundaries to safeguard quality time**

You can plan and then other activities come up and you realize they also need your attention. You have to be principled enough not to interfere with time set apart to be with your child. You have to ensure activities with your child are hardly cancelled. That way, your child will know he/she is unparalleled and that you are ready to sacrifice anything to ascertain his/her welfare.

e) Keep away pressing assignments
There is a strong persuasion to carry work while on holiday or during time set apart to be with your child. Leave your computers and tablets at home, so that they do not get in the way of time together. This may be understandable since there maybe assignments that require your attention, however, it is upon you to be decisive regarding not meddling with your set time with your child. Other things can indeed wait.

Chapter 5

ChaPTEr fivE
Child aBuSE

Behind every person who has committed an unimaginable crime is an adult who committed unimaginable violence against them as a child. All of them, as if it was plotted that way. Violence begets violence, and that

violence
begets even more violence
Ji-young gong

The above quote highlights the trans-generational nature of abuse. When one person is abused, he/she in turn abuses another, and this other person takes it out on another person. This cycle has to be reversed and it can effectively be done at the parenting level if parents are well informed about parenting. Ingrained within the abuser is deep seated resentment, rage, frustration, hate and other negative feelings that eventually get released to undeserving victims.

Abused children during childhood years are a liability to a nation if they have not healed from the trauma. Trauma emanating from childhood has a way of stunting the emotional, psychological and spiritual growth of a child. Such a child is not able to release his/her potential to achieve maximum results in life. Many times such children get limited through self-doubt, shame and a distressing mistrust of people and the world. They move through life halfheartedly because they are not able to loose themselves to a world they consider hostile and unsafe. They are waiting for the worst to happen to them and therefore cannot release their full potential. If they do, they do it aggressively which again turns against them eventually. Hence, these children are not able to give back to their nation the way they would have desired if their mental health was not harmed.

Again, children who are abused have a tendency of having a revenge mission. They tell themselves, "I will do to others what was done to me." It is not a conscious but an unconscious decision coming from unresolved childhood traumas. The experiences of abuse whether episodic or recurrent instill feelings of unfairness in the survivor. There is a relationship between unresolved child abuse traumas and criminality. A big number of inmates in jails are there because of committing crimes under the influence of unresolved childhood traumas. That is why child abuse should not be taken lightly. As a nation, we might be incubating terror and criminality if we do not help children deal with issues of abuse and neglect adequately. We can save our Kenyan shilling by taking good care of our children by humanizing them for positive future prospects.

The meaning of Child abuse

There are many ways to describe child abuse and neglect, as it is a broad and wide-ranging problem that affects children all over the globe. It entails anything, which individuals or institutions do or fail to do which directly or indirectly harms a child or damages his or her prospects of safe and healthy development into adulthood. We can also say that child abuse is an act of commission or omission that harms the child physically, socially, emotionally and psychologically. This indeed is a violation and infringement of a child's rights and needs.

1 Timothy 5:8 cautions, *"Anyone who does not provide for their relatives, and especially for their own household, has denied the faith and is worse than an unbeliever."* This means that our being Christians obligates us to take responsibility of the nurture and provision of our households, especially children. You should be aware of people who can violate your child including parents, siblings, grandparents, uncles, aunts, house helps, neighbors, teachers, strangers, pastors, among others. You ought to be alive to the fact that anyone can abuse your child so that you can cushion him/her from harm. We need our children whole and complete, not having dents that make them incapable of participating in life fully.

Parents, guardians and other caregivers should ensure children's best interests are guarded during all stages of development. In Kenya, child protection rules are currently not being fully implemented. Compliance with such legislation would increase with the awareness of the magnitude of the problem and the factors that put children at risk. As a parent, awareness about abuse and neglect would help you put measures that provide protection and security for your child. Such knowledge will inform you about effective intervention measures if abuse is meted on your child.

State of Child abuse in Kenya

Findings from the 2010 Kenya Violence Against Children Survey (KVACS) carried out under the Ministry of Gender, Children and Social Development together with other partners indicated that violence against children is a serious problem in Kenya. The study sampled 3,000 young people and showed that levels of violence prior to age 18 as reported by 18 to 24 year olds (lifetime experiences) indicated that during childhood, 32% of females and 18% of males had experienced sexual violence. 66% of females and 73% of males had experienced physical violence and 26% of females and 32% of males had experienced emotional violence as children. 13% of females and 9% of males had experienced all three types of violence during childhood.

The report notes that, "Most worrisome was that violence against children did not appear to be random or uncoordinated, or perpetuated by strangers. The abusers are not only known to their victims but often have close, personal ties. This means that a child is most often beaten, slapped or hit by a parent or even most often sexually abused by a romantic partner or boyfriend or girlfriend, or even a family member. The consequences of this violence can be lasting and enduring for both the victims and communities as a whole. Victims of childhood violence are more likely to engage in risky behaviors such as drug and alcohol abuse, sexual relationships with multiple partners and unprotected sex. Young women are more likely to become pregnant with unwanted pregnancies and the risks of exposure to sexually transmitted diseases, such as HIV/AIDS, are considerably higher."

Abuse of children is preventable through educating the caregivers on effects of abuse on children's emotional health, relationships and personality development. As a parent, you should be clear about causes of abuse, forms of abuse and ways of protecting your child from abuse. You have to be alert to situations that can predispose your child to abuse. Abuse harms and distorts children's reality thus interfering with their normal development.

Robina's Case
Robina loved her dad and could not leave his side when she was small. Her mother was a nurse in one of the national hospitals and used to work at night. When she worked at night, Robina and her siblings were taken care of by a male neighbor who was to keep vigil because the father came home late from his drinking sprees. This neighbor started having sex with Robina at age

*4 and banned her from ever telling anyone. Robina kept the secret fearing
that the neighbor would harm her if she dared tell anyone. After form
four,she had her first episode of depression and she had severe
hallucinations. Her mother took her to hospital and she somehow was well.*

*After that, her mother's boyfriend, 82 years of age approached her and told
her he wanted a relationship with her. She was dazed because she had
always called him uncle. She told her brother who just silently walked away.
She then told her mother who told her not to disappoint 'uncle.'*

*Robina soon started having sex with the 'uncle', which she did not enjoy.
During that time, she was a born again Christian who sang in the choir.
These two conflicting lifestyles gave her intense conflicts but she did not
know what to do. She had other boyfriends, but the mother's boyfriend was
the consistent sexual partner. She had started binging heavily and she was in
some way losing it. She wanted so much to stop having irresponsible sex and
drinking but she could not manage. When she listened to herself, she could
tell the neighbor set her up.*

Robina like other neglected children was prone to abuse. Like in other cases,
a caregiver in the form of a neighbor took advantage of her and cautioned her
never to disclose the secret. Children feel they have little or no power over
adults; adults therefore should know better and shield children. Robina had to
live with her dirty secret until the time she attended counselling. It was
painful to recall these repressed experiences, which buried terrifying
emotions. She needed a counselling approach, which was purely
nonjudgmental for her to start daring to unravel her trauma. When she
eventually did, she cut off those harmful relations and stopped drinking.
Now, she is a successful entrepreneur who funds programs whose
beneficiaries are girls who are sexually molested. Nevertheless, it is
important to note that many such cases go unreported and many victims have
to live with the ugly consequences of the abuse throughout their lives.

forms of abuse
There are manyforms of abuse meted on children as pointed out byKVACS.
Some of the prevalent forms of abuse include physical, emotional, and sexual
abuse, neglect and abandonment, bullying, abduction and child labor.

Type of Abuse Definition Signs

Physical
Normally carried out in the name of discipline and punishment,
especially by
parents, guardians and other
caregivers
This type of abuse involves caning, battering, pinching, slapping, punching, burning with (water, fire, cigarette
butts), kicking, scolding shaking a child, etc

NB: It is important to note that disciplining involves teaching, instructing, coaching, mentoring or tutoring. Disciplining does not mean punishing a child for stepping out of line, but teaching him or her the way he or she should go.
Whip or cane marks, pinch marks, burns, bite marks, bleeding and bruises, injuries on the head, hand or back, absence from school or truancy, compliant behavior or over submissiveness, frequently running away from home, general fear of adults, fear of returning home, poorly
healed bones, fractures or dislocations, deterioration in work performance, aggression, resentment and violent
behavior, and bed-wetting.

Emotional Abuse This type of abuse has

an adverse effect on the behavioral, perceptual or emotional development of a child. What could lead to emotional abuse includes humiliation, verbal insults, derogatory language and making unattainable demands on children.
Feelings of insecurity, attention seeking, withdrawal from friends or physical isolation, refusal to speak or communicate, eating disorders (eating too much or lack of appetite), bed wetting, aggressive or violent behavior, compulsive stealing, alcohol and substance abuse, sleeping disorders (insomnia or nightmares), depression, low self-esteem or lack of
self-confidence, poor school performance, apprehension or unnatural fear, biting nails or thumb sucking, self-harm or suicide attempts.
Sexual Abuse Sexual abuse is any sort of nonconsensual sexual contact. It is any sexual act with a child performed by an adult or an older child.

Child sexual abuse includes but is not limited to fondling any part of the body, clothed or unclothed, penetrative sex, including penetration of the mouth, encouraging a child to engage in sexual activity including masturbation,
intentionally engaging in sexual activity in front of a child, showing children pornography or using children to create pornography and encouraging a child to engage in prostitution.
Noticeable fear of a particular person or certain places,
unusual response from the child when asked if he or she was touched, unreasonable fear of physical examination, drawings that show sexual acts, abrupt changes in behavior, such as bed-wetting or losing control of his or her bowels, sudden awareness of genitals and sexual acts and words and attempting to get other children to perform sexual acts.
Neglect and This refers to the failure of Abandonment a parent or other person

charged with responsibility over a child to provide the child with necessities of life like food, shelter, clothing, medical care and education, as a result of which that child's physical, emotional, mental, psychological, social and intellectual development is put at risk.
Dirty skin, disease and lice infection, inappropriate and/ or inadequate clothing, poor personal hygiene,

constant tiredness, malnourishment and being underweight, illness due to deficiencies such as anemia and kwashiorkor, frequent lateness or absence from school (truancy), low self-esteem and poor social relationships.

Neglect and abandonment also happen when a child is denied love and emotional support. Consequently, the child develops low self-worth because he or she does not perceive himself or herself as important.

Such children tend to develop internal conflicts because of their feelings of abandonment, and they are not able to
develop a healthy identity. As adults, they may exhibit childish behavior if their dependency needs were not met, such as craving for approval, admiration and celebration of their
uniqueness.

A child also gets abandoned through female genital
mutilation (FGM), forced
early marriages, gender
discrimination, customary and religious rituals (sacrificial killings), stigmatization (for instance of HIV/AIDS orphans, disabled children or unwanted babies).

Bullying This refers to the use of force, authority, privilege or power to frighten or injure others by hitting, taking a person's things, name-calling, cyber shaming or racial slur. Bullying happens to those under-privileged by age, status level and deficient when it comes to skills.
Constant fear and anxiety, low academic performance, isolation and insecurity, low self-worth, aggression, suicidal ideas and being quick to get angry.

Abduction It entails taking a child away without the child's willingness and permission from the custodian/guardian. Abduction can be carried out by members of the child's family or by strangers. Abduction by a family member mostly occurs when parents are separated or divorced. Such parental or familial child abduction may lead to parental alienation, a form of child abuse that entails disconnecting a child from a targeted parent and maligned side of the family.

Abduction or kidnapping by strangers (people outside the family, natural or legal guardians) is done with any of the following motives:

a) Extortion, to elicit ransom from the guardians for the child's return

b) Illegal adoption, where a stranger steals a child with the intent to rear them as their own or to sell to a prospective adoptive parent

c) Human trafficking, where a stranger steals a child with the intention of exploiting the child themselves or by trade for any of the possible abuses, including slavery, forced labor, sexual abuse, or even illegal organ trading .

d) Murder
Effects of abduction include anxiety, trauma, depression, feeling of insecurity and fear. Child Labor
Child labor refers to the

engagement of persons below the age of 18 in the labor force to the detriment of their mental, physical, moral, social and vocational development.

It is perpetrated under the cover of supplementing family income, self-support, and being useful.

Examples of child labor include cattle herding, child prostitution, hiring children as domestic workers, hawking, begging for money, involving children in baby care, car washing, child soldiers, fetching water and firewood, garbage collecting, and working in farms/plantations.

Difference between child labor and child work
Child work is healthy because it is a social process of
developing work competence in a child, whereas child labor is abuse because it disrespects the child's abilities and needs.

Child labor jeopardizes health, human dignity, education and the economic situation of the child. In child labor, the child's dependency needs are ignored. These include attention,
protection, guidance and
nurturance.

Effects of abuse For children, trauma caused by abuse is stored somatically (in the body) or emotionally because their brains are not developed enough to process the trauma.

Tiredness, scratches/wounds/ bruises, stunted growth/frail body, occupational diseases and injuries, dropping out of school, lost opportunities in life, physical injuries, illness or diseases associated with the jobs done, poor performance in school, poor social
relationships, psychological or behavioral disorders, lack of confidence and low self-esteem.

Sadi's Case
Sadi, eight years old, is an eloquent girl who has learnt to reason like an adult. She is caught up in a court tussle regarding her custody that she so much wishes would be sorted out soonest. She prefers to stay with dad because, according to her, he was consistently there for her whereas her mum disappeared frequently. In one court session, she told the magistrate she preferred to be taken to an orphanage rather than stay with her mother. She recalls watching her mother raving mad and breaking things in the house. She once told her mother, "I do not need you to take care of me because you left me when I needed you most." The mother accused her husband of brain washing Sadi against her. One time during a court case, the legal officers took hold of Sadi and hurdled her into her mother's vehicle by force. She cried bitterly about the unfairness and felt brutally disconnected from her dad. Because of the undeserved experiences, she wants to study law in future so that she can protect the custodial rights of children by ensuring that children get what they prefer.

Sadi's case brings out common scenarios in court-rooms in the 21st century. As parents haggle for adoption rights, the core needs of the child are disregarded. Most parents are simply self-seeking, wanting to win the battle, but not for the long-term benefit of the child.

Kellen's Case
Kellen was taken on board at 10 years by Julie, her married sister who, henceforth, supported her in education and upkeep. She was in standard six when Julie's husband started touching her breasts, remarking that they looked like ripe fruits. He then proceeded to make suggestive moves and one day he entered her room and raped her. That night, she could not sleep because of pain and she bled profusely. He warned her never ever to tell anybody and pinched her thigh to demonstrate what would happen if she dared reveal their secret. It weighed so heavily on her that one day she shared her experiences with her sister who in response shouted at her, calling her a prostitute. She went on to beat her until she was unconscious. After that incident, Julie's husband continued having sex with Kellen until she completed form four. Every time he had sex with her, he would tell her that she was the one who brought herself to him like many harlots do. At 45 years, Kellen had to go through counselling following severe depression, emanating from those years of physical, emotional and sexual abuse.

Kellen's case illustrates how abuse meted on children can be manysided. Kellen was emotionally and sexually molested by a relative; hence, the impact was wide-ranging. The trauma from the incestuous acts ended up becoming an ingredient that contributed to Kellen's personality disposition. Notice she became a depressed woman who had to spend her life seeking treatment. After all the struggles, Kellen decided to work out her issues and be happy and fulfilled.

William's Case
William, now 21 years, has become panicky, anxious and prone to emotional breakdowns. On the face, he is a strong, successful, and intelligent young man whom many admire. Life was hard as he grew up since his parents were always fighting and later separated. William had a younger sister he protected but he always felt uncared for. He was taken to boarding school while in standard five against his will and the parents hardly ever visited him. During the holidays, he stayed with an aunt who made him clean the house, the compound and clothes for all those who were part of the

household. He recalls being bullied in school and this reinforced the feeling of abandonment. Now, he feels like one who is trapped in a cave that is dark and that has no exit. He wishes someone breaks the door open and delivers him from his loneliness, helplessness, disorientation, depression and panic. He now understands this situation emanates from his childhood developmental needs that were not met. He also wonders, "What makes me take care of everyone else, but I do not allow myself to be taken care of."

William is seeking to understand himself because he has manyconflicts within. When his parents were fighting, they could not have been available emotionally for him; hence, he was emotionally malnourished. When he was made to work for adults, his needs for protection, provision and nurturance were not met. As an adult, he takes care of others but does not allow others to take care of him because he never learnt to receive love and attention as a child. He was always the giver.

Causes of Child abuse
The following are situations that predispose a child to abuse:

• Children left in the custody of male adults, step-parents, step-children and grandparents
• Orphaned children
• Children with disabilities
• Children caught up in conflict ridden marriages and families
• Children growing up in polygamous families
• Children suffering mental illnesses
• Children having personality disorders
• Children who are ignorant about what abuse constitutes
• Children suffering poverty
• Children who are meek and timid
• Street children
• Children living in congested housing
• Children brought up by irresponsible parents
• Children coming from broken families

interventions in Situations of Child abuse and Neglect There are various interventions that are crucial in situations of child abuse and neglect, namely, psychosocial interventions, legal interventions and parent/guardian interventions.

Psychosocial Interventions Legal Interventions Parent/Guardian Interventions

a. Provision of
counseling services
b. Provision of
medical intervention services
c. Strengthening the already existing family life education
d. Closely monitoring and supervising service providers
e. Effective distribution and utilization of resources at all levels
f. Continuous
provision of service providers and
caregivers
g. If possible
removing the child from the harmful environment
h. Empowering
families by creating awareness of the negative effects of abuse
i. Providing family support
j. Starting school feeding programs
k. Provision of training on child abuse
l. Ensuring provision of affordable
education
m. Planning follow up for abuse victims
a. Reporting
immediately
to the area
children's officer, police station, or organizations dealing with
children's rights
b. Preserving
evidence for legal action
c. Raising
awareness of
children's rights
d. Ensuring the
establishment of child abuse reporting desks
e. Strengthening and empowering local administrations on child abuse
f. Seeking
community
support
g. Promoting
children's rights
h. Creation of child friendly systems, e.g. police, courts
i. Creating
neighborhood networks
a. Loving,
protecting
and caring for your child
b. Providing
counseling and guidance to your child

c. Providing
food, shelter and clothing to your child
d. Creating time for your child
e. Supervising your child
f. Creating a conducive environment for proper
growth and development
g. Avoiding
humiliating a child
h. Being a good listener to a child
i. Coaching
children on life skills

Parents Empowerment

The Bible in Hosea 4:6 says, *"My people are destroyed from lack of knowledge…"* Cases of child abuse and neglect are prevalent in the world today and when we allow our children to be harmed, we destroy future generations. Some people cope with child abuse by engaging in alcoholism, sex addiction etc. That is why it is important for victims of child abuse to receive counselling so that they purge themselves from hopeless living.

Parents and society require relevant information to protect children from abuse and neglect. As a parent, you need to continually update yourself with relevant information regarding child abuse. This information can be disseminated through various forums like media, focused trainings, workshops and seminars. Focused trainings (including training on effective parenting with diverse facilitative methods like watching videos, demonstrations, role-plays and discussions) equip parents and other caregivers to be alert to issues of child abuse and neglect. Such information include types and signs of abuse and neglect and appreciation that anyone can be an abuser. This helps parents detect, assess and respond appropriately to issues of child abuse and neglect.

Chapter 6

ChaPTEr Six
diSCiPliNE aNd COrrECTiON fOr ChildrEN

If we don't shape our kids, they will be shaped by outside forces that don't care what shape our kids are in.
dr. louise hart

discipline

Pertinent family investments should be channeled towards developing wholesome, grounded and disciplined children. As a parent, if you are reluctant or unskillful in developing basic disciplines in your children; inner emptiness and garbage from external quarters will fill the gaps. Correctly disciplining your children is an important skill that all parents need to learn. Proverbs 19:18 state, *"Discipline your children, for in that there is hope; do not be a willing party to their death."* The Bible is warning us that if as parents we do not discipline our children, we are colluding in their destruction. However, discipline is not the same as correction, although correction can be used as means of inculcating discipline.

Discipline entails teaching your children what is right, what is wrong, how to respect the rights of others, and which behaviors are acceptable and which ones are not, with the objective of raising children who feel secure, loved, self-confident, self-disciplined and are able to control whims.A disciplined child is not overly frustrated by the normal stresses of everyday life. Children have different *temperaments* at different levels of development, so a style of discipline that may work with a particular child may fail to produce desirable results in another.
As a parent, you should understand that the way you behave when disciplining your child can either produce positive or negative effects. Your child may look at you and pick resentment and hatred. The child may interpret the discipline as rejection and not being good enough. If you withdraw the discipline after your child protests, becomes violent or launches into temper tantrums, then your child will see your lack of sureness and may start manipulating you. However, if you are firm and consistent, then your child will learn that it does not pay to fight because in the end he/she must do what he/she was protesting against anyway. In addition, you should be *consistent* in your methods of discipline and how you implement them. This

applies to all caregivers, not just parents. It is normal for children to test the caregiver's limits, and if you are inconsistent in correction, then you will be inadvertently encouraging more acts of bad behavior.

Tamera's Case
Tamera cannot remember a time her parents taught her to do things the right way. She was expected to know how to care of her younger siblings, supervise them, instill discipline in them, cook, serve and clean after them. She despised undertaking all these chores and felt deeply neglected and misused. However, she always wondered why she felt that way about her parents. They were adored in the village for disciplining their children? She wished her parents could understand her longing for instruction and direction but she never received any of that. She remembers many times her mother came home and shouted at her, called her names and pinched her long and hard. She somehow thought that even discipline should be realistic and used to teach good behavior. Nevertheless, this was not the case with her parents. She always wondered who would educate her parents. She is now 30 years old and a mother of two, she is so ruthless and high handed with them. Her children shirk away from her the same way she did her parents. Are they cursed as a family, she wonders.

Tamera is disadvantaged because her parents are lacking in providing helpful discipline and correction. They do not realize they should coach Tamera on tasks they require her to carry out. Their way of dispensing correction is ill informed and harmful. They should help her understand her wrongs and apply a correction measure that is proportionate to the wrong committed. That way, she will have faith in her parents and appreciate that all they do is meant to make her a better person.

Planning for Children's discipline

decide what you want your child to learn through disciplining him/her : Disciplining actually means teaching. Let it be clear in your mind what you want your child to know, whether it is a skill, desirable values or societal norms.

in disciplining, take into account the age, temperament and personality of the child: Children, even those coming from the same family are different.

The discipline techniques you apply to one child may therefore, not work for another child

for consistency, develop a list showing unacceptable behavior and the corresponding punishment: ensure that the consequences match the undesirable behavior in terms of seriousness. For example, do not take away phone privileges from your child for a year if he or she forgets to take out the trash only once. This would be excessively punitive.

discuss the correction plan with your child, if he or she is old enough to give his/her input: Find out what he or she thinks is fair and what is unfair about the plan, and explain how and why you came up with those specific rules and consequences.

acknowledge good behavior: List appropriate behaviors and attach a reward to each of them. Discuss this part of the discipline plan too with your child.

Pick your battles: Do not get upset over every little breach. Learn to ignore some of your child's misbehaviors and negative habits. **Keep communication open:**Talk with your child to find out why he or she chose to break a rule, or why he or she decided not to comply with your instructions.Then brainstorm to find out ways of reaching a compromise.

Be flexible with your discipline: As your child grows up, you will need to make changes to the disciplining plan to reflect the child's age, personality and circumstances. Discuss this with your child as you choose the rewards and consequences.

make your plan unique: If you have more than one child, create an individual discipline plan for each of them.Whether you have 3 children or 13, each plan should reflect his or her individuality.

forgive yourself if you make a mistake: You are human, and it is normal to find yourself yelling at your children occasionally. Do not abandon all your hard work over one mistake; it helps if you can tell your child you are sorry you lost your temper. Do not make children take responsibility of your emotional outbursts by making them feel guilty for it. Just revisit your discipline plan, make adjustments if necessary, and continue following it.

always show respect to your child. Even when you are disciplining him or her, make sure he or she understands that you love and respect him/ her. Your child's behavior may leave much to be desired, but he/she is human nevertheless given to omissions, rebellion and going overboard sometimes.

Effective discipline and Correction

Your child needs you to be his or her parent, not his or her peer. Hopefully, you do not feel the need for your youngster to like you every minute; parents who have this need are destined to be ineffective, frustrated, and disappointed. Just by saying no, you will clarify who is in charge, set the boundaries, create the values, and show the parental guidance children want and need. Children need to be loved and to love; therefore, it is necessary to correct the wrong done but not blame or criticize the child, which may make him or her feel ashamed, useless and undeserving of love.

Correction is an important element in any effort that is aimed at changing a child's behavior. It should never be punishment but a correction measure meant to develop a child to be better. There are various types of correction measures and the one chosen must fit the need or the deed. While children have a need for parental control, that control should vary for different ages, in different situations or stages of development. The form of discipline you use with a six-year-old may not work or be appropriate when that child is ten.

Children may feel guilty about inappropriate behavior or failing to do the right thing, and a mild, appropriate correction often relieves them of that guilt. Like everyone else, children have the right to make mistakes and learn from their experience.

Basics on Effective discipline and Correction

Stay calm, do not be carried away when your child misbehaves: Avoid yelling and screaming, since this can teach your child that it is alright to lose control if you do not get your way. If you feel like anger is getting the better of you, then take a break until you can regain your composure.

avoid too much criticism: Make sure your child understands that it is the misbehavior that you are unhappy with and that you will always love him or her. Criticism makes the child devalue him/herself.

avoid too much praise: You do not need to continuously praise your child, especially for routine activities, because it will make your comments less effective.

do not focus on negatives all the time: Focus more on what your child should do and what good he/she has done, especially when offering positive reinforcement. It is much better to say, "I like that you put all your clothes away,"instead of saying,"I like that at long last,you finally got around to putting your clothes away without my asking."

avoid physical punishment as much as possible: Spanking has never been shown to be more effective than other correction measures and will make your child more aggressive and angry.

remember to give rewards and praise for good behavior: Giving rewards (verbal and physical) reinforces certain behaviors that are desirable and discourages behaviors that are undesirable.

understand the difference between rewards and bribes: A reward is something your child receives after he/she has done something helpful, whereas a bribe is given beforehand to try and motivate your child to do what you want. Bribes should be avoided.

Be a good role model: Set an example of certain behaviors that you would want your child to emulate, for example, talking to others with respect or working hard to complete a task or participating in teamwork.

Provide your child with a safe environment: Create an environment in which he/she feels secure and loved.Therefore,workat zapping conflict in the home by avoiding quarreling or arguing with your spouse, friend or neighbor in your children's presence.

Common forms of Correction

There are common ways of correcting children, which parents usually utilize including:

a. giving postive attention: Giving your child attention regularly; for example doing activities with him or her, observing him/her as he/she engages in activities will make a child assign worth to self. Attention deficiency makes a child look for attention inappropriately, which may eventually make a child develop undesirable behaviors.

c. give positive feedback: Catch your child engaging in helpful value adding activities and validate your child. This will make your child know what is permissible and acceptable and what is not. It also boosts a child's self-esteem.

d. give rewards: Giving rewards is a good way of instilling positive habits. This will help your child develop a code of conduct that is self-enhancing.

e. Orientation and coaching: Orientation provides a child with relevant information to respond adequately to unfamiliar situations and experiences. An example of this would be preparing a child for what he/she will experience when he/she joins a new school. Coaching has to do with instilling skills for example hand washing after visiting the toilet.

f. ignore inappropriate habits: if you ignore some of your child's attention seeking habits, your child will stop exhibiting them.

g. remove privileges: You can remove a privilege that your child had before. You can take away visits for some time if your child has not been honoring agreed upon time for returning home.

h. getting a child to make amends: Help your child to examine his/her mistakes and determine where he/she went wrong. It is a levelheaded critical examination of one's mistakes. This will help your child develop understanding and sensitivity for other people. The child has to acknowledge the importance of relating with those that he/she has wronged in caring ways. Eventually, the child offers his/her apology. If your child had taken another child's item, he/she should return that item to the owner. Likewise, if your child had lost another child's item, he/she should repay. That way, your child will learn responsible co-existence

i. law of natural consequences: You should help your child appreciate the law of natural consequences. He/she should be helped to acknowledge that certain feelings, thoughts and decisions have predetermined consequences.

For example, teasing playmates may, for instance, cause your child to lose his/her friends, get hit, or get teased.

j. logical Consequences: In certain situations, a natural consequence may be too dangerous. For instance, bike riding in the street may result in an accident or injury. So, it is advisable you provide a correction or consequence that appears logical and demonstrates a reasonable relationship between the behavior and the consequence. For example, if a child rides his or her bicycle in a busy street, he/she could be made to lose the use of the bike for a week.

k. Behavioral Penalty: You can give moderated correction in response to behavior for which there is no natural or logical consequence. However, the penalty should be something meaningful to the child. For instance, when a child does not care for his or her items, he or she may lose outing privileges. These behavioral penalties should be calmly discussed before they are instituted. Rules and expectations should be clear, preferably laid out in advance, not presented as a surprise, a threat, or punishment.

l. Time-out: This is a behavior change technique, which involves briefly separating your child from an environment where he/she committed the unacceptable behavior. If your child has slapped another child, you can tell your child to go and sit or stand in a particular place, away from the rest of the children. Hence, this is an effective way of dealing with your child's impulsive, aggressive, or hostile behavior, which often includes hitting, having tantrums, throwing valuable items like toys, name-calling, whining, interrupting, humiliating, or directly disobeying a request to stop a particular action. Timeout is not useful for a child whose only recognizable problem behavior is excessive sulking, crying, or whining. For these children, it is important to discover the root or purpose of these behaviors. You have to make sure you are not making your child feel unwanted and useless. You are aiming at the child realizing the particular behavior is unacceptable or even hurtful. Often a corner (hence the common term *corner time*) or a similar space where the child is to stand or sit during timeouts is designated. Evaluate to ensure lessons are learnt from the method.

m. Scolding and verbal expression of disapproval: Use this approach sparingly and only when you as the parent are in charge of your own emotions. This kind of correction should be applied soon after the undesirable behavior and focus on the particular bad behavior. Scolding should never be done in a nagging, humiliating, cynical, or sarcastic manner, which can result in the child feeling shame and resentment. The problem of the actual behavior may get "lost" in this turbulent emotional climate. Parental anger is normal, but it should not be excessive or un-proportional to what the child did to provoke it. Always respect your child's dignity when you scold or communicate disapproval. For example, "I don't like what you do to your cousins at all; you are so mean to them. Allow yourself to be kind to others."

n. Physical Correction: Parents often ask, "Should I spank my child?" Spanking is an overused method of correction by many caregivers including parents. For instance, if your child runs out into the street, you may sweep the child up and in a moment of anxiety about the child's well-being spank him/her due to the anxiety you experience in the spur of the moment. In such a case, it is the parent's expression of disapproval, not the spanking that is an effective deterrent.

Spanking may relieve your frustration as a parent for the moment and extinguish the undesirable behavior for a short time. However, it is the least effective way to correct a child. It is harmful emotionally to you and your child. Not only can it result in physical harm,it could also teach your child that violence is an acceptable way to discipline or express anger.While it could stop the undesirable behavior temporarily, spanking does not teach alternative behavior. It also interferes with the development of trust, a sense of security, and effective communication, since spanking takes the place of communication. It may also cause emotional pain and resentment.

Effective versus ineffective Correction
Effective Correction

Effective correction is a deterrent measure, aimed at the behavior, not the person. It accomplishes five things:

a) Reinforces appropriate behavior and serves as a deterrent for negative behavior

b) Helps the child differentiate between appropriate and inappropriate behavior
c) Reinforces the instructions given
d) Makes the child develop the habit of behaving appropriately to avoid pain, leading to a disciplined child
e) Communicates care and security

Guide to Effective Correction

a) Make sure that the rules and demands are reasonable by listening to what the child says

b) Wait until both you and the child are in control of the anger before correcting him or her

c) Make the child see why what he or she did is wrong
d) If the child is sorry, negotiate so that a solution that satisfies both of you is arrived at
e) If the child does not accept the mistake, explain as simply and as briefly as possible why it is wrong and then apply the correction
f) Make sure that the mode of correction is proportionate to the age of the child and gravity of the mistake

Ineffective Correction

It is penalty that is not very well thought out; it can be too lenient, too extreme or it may not be appropriate for the wrongs done by the child.
Ineffective correction accomplishes five things:

a) Satisfies the person doing the correcting
b) Often produces immediate results but may hurt the child
c) Makes the child develop ways of not being caught while continuing with inappropriate behavior.
d) Makes the child insensitive to the unpleasantness of the correction over time, becoming hardened to the extent where he or she chooses to be punished in exchange for the joy of misbehaving
e) Makes the child feel devalued and dehumanized

Effects of Inappropriate Correction

a) May cause bruises, swellings and fractures
b) May cause death
c) May cause scars which remain as reminders of past brutality
d) May result to low self-esteem, leading to psychological problems
e) May result to poor performance due to fear of trying and failing
f) May cause hard feelings, becoming a source of serious indiscipline problems
g) May harden the child, thus making correction to be of no effect
h) Your child may emulate your acts of violence, making him or her adopt it in in his/her life as standard behavior

memo from your Child

Don't spoil me; I know quite well that I ought not have all that I ask for; I'm only testing you.

Don't be afraid to be firm with me; I prefer it. It makes me feel more secure.

Don't let me form bad habits; I have to rely on you to detect them in the early stages.

Don't make me feel smaller than I am; It only makes me behave stupid and foolish.

Don't correct me in front of people if you can help it. Don't make me feel that my mistakes are sins; it upsets my set of values. Don't be upset when I say "I hate you," it's not you I hate, but your power to hinder.

Don't protect me from consequences; I need to learn the painful way sometimes.

Don't nag; if you do; I will need to protect myself by appearing deaf. Don't make rash promises; remember I feel badly let down when promises are broken.

Don't tax my honesty too much; I am easily frightened into telling lies. Don't be inconsistent; that completely confuses me and makes me lose faith in you. Don't tell me my fears are silly; they are terribly real to me and you can do much to reassure me if you try to understand. Don't ever suggest that you are perfect or infallible; It gives me too great a shock when I discover that you are neither.

Don't forget that I can't thrive without lots of love and understanding; but I don't need to tell you that; do I?

Anonymous Author

Chapter 7

ChaPTEr SEvEN
dEaliNg wiTh COmmON BEhaviOr PrOBlEmS

Each day of our lives, we make deposits in the memory banks of our children
Charles r. Swindoll

Naturally,humans have tendencies for self-nurturance,self-preservation and self-destruction. Children require positive socialization so that they can fit in the real world, to be self-nurturing and self-preserving. Through socialization, parents program their children's mental hard disks that guide their life's ideologies, decisions, choices and actions. Every parent's greatest dread is his or her child turning out to be unable to achieve goals at personal, social and vocational levels. This means that as a parent, you need to help your child be skilled enough to face life's issues and challenges competently. Some common behavioral problems your child may have include, irresponsibility, being disrespectful, social difficulties, dishonesty, selfishness, lacking self-control, defiance, misuse of money, addiction to mass media and sibling rivalry.

irresponsibility
This is failure to give enough attention and thought to what one is doing. It also describes a lack of interest or effort in particular things. Children have these tendencies because they have limited mental abilities to perceive, comprehend, process adequately and respond to particular information. Hence, many times, your growing child may be innocently irresponsible. As a result, a child may end up in frequent failure and a life marked by disorder.

Instilling Responsibility
a. Consider your child's age, exposure and experience before giving responsibilities.
b. Establish rules pertaining to handling things and situations.

They should be consistent and followed by everyone at home. c. Supervise your child as much as necessary when handling
things that require care, and reward him or her for the rules
adhered to once the activity is over.
d. Show your child how to care for everything he/she is supposed
to handle and model care for him or her.

e. When your child is careless or irresponsible, explain to him or
her exactly what he or she is doing wrong and what should be
done and why.
f. Let the child experience the natural consequences of behaving
carelessly or irresponsibly. Make sure he or she sees the direct
connection between the behavior and consequences. g. Write a contract with
your child regarding the specific,careless
and irresponsible behaviors he or she is engaging in. h. Draw a timetable of
the work the child is supposed to do and
supervise the implementation. Make sure your child has enough
time for play in the schedule.
i. Make sure your child has enough room when required to sit or
work with things that involve breakables.
j. Make sure there is a designated place for all items and always
see to it that your child adheres to the rule of keeping things
where they are supposed to be.
k. Separate things that are fragile from those that cannot break
easily.

Being disrespectful
This is failure to acknowledge the value and dignity of others. A disrespectful
child acts in ways that reduce the worth of others. This is manifested in
behaviors such as interrupting others as they talk, arguing with senior people,
being rude, using obscene language, not giving others their rightful space,
and insensitivity to other people's feelings.

Pius' Case
The principal of Kianga Boys Secondary School looked sternly at Pius'
parents and blurted out, "You are the kind of parents who should not have
had a child in the first place.How do you allow your son to be a brat who
cannot fit in any social set up? I am tired of dealing with cases connected to
Pius. I wonder why you are unable to bring up your only child. Pius is the
most irresponsible, careless, defiant, disrespectful, dishonest, selfish and
anti-social boy I have ever handled in my entire teaching career. You give
him a lot of pocket money; I hear he is even a marijuana dealer in the school.
Have you ever set rules for Pius to follow? He asked me yesterday what right
I have to impose rules on him when he is a free individual."

Pius' mother broke down and bemoaned that the principal hates Pius. The husband sighed heavily and told her, "I am tired of the way you keep protecting Pius in the name of love; we have to do something as his parents." The principal looked at them, turned and walked away, seemingly weary and disgusted.

Pius is a perfect case of a child who is not taught sensitivity for others and boundary marking when it comes to dos and don'ts with other people and situations. He does not have respect for the elderly like his principal.Certainly,he will find it verydifficult to survive in a real world of expectations. Pius' parents lack a jointly agreed upon parenting strategy of dealing with Pius misbehaviors. His mother has destructive love for her son, which does not allow him to go through natural pain and struggle to be disciplined. Clearly, Pius' parents' marriage is in turmoil.

Teaching Your Child Good Manners

It is normal for you as a parent to expect your child to be courteous; after all,your child's behavior reflects you.Good manners come easilyto some children, while others struggle. Understanding what constitutes good manners will help you teach your child good manners. Good manners are necessary for your child to co-exist with others in the world.

Expect respect: The root of good manners is respect for other people, and the root of respect is sensitivity. The sensitive child will naturally become respectful because he or she cares for the other person's feelings. In recent years, it has become socially correct to teach children to be assertive. Actually being assertive is healthy so long as it does not override politeness and good manners.

Teach Polite words Early: Children as young as two years old can learn to say words like 'please', 'excuse me' and 'thank you'. Even though they may not yet understand the social implications of these words, the toddler will become aware that saying please is how you get what you want and thank you is how you end an interaction. Even before the child grasps the meaning of these words, he or she learns they are important because mum and dad use them a lot, and they have such nice expressions on their faces when they say these words.

model manners: From age two to four, what a child hears, the child repeats. Therefore, if you want your child to acquire good manners, let him or her hear you say words such as please, thank you, you are welcome, and excuse me from you as you interact with people.

acknowledge the Child: When you and your child are in a crowd of adults, tuning out your child is asking for trouble. Even a child who is usually well behaved will become a nuisance in order to break through to you. Including the child teaches social skills, and acknowledging his or her presence shows him/her that he/she is valued. Therefore, stay connected with your child in situations that put him/her at risk for undesirable behavior. During a visit with other adults, keep your younger child physically close to you (or you stay close to him/her) and maintain frequent verbal and eye contact. Help your older child feel part of the action so that he/she is less likely to get bored and wander into trouble.

do Not force good manners: When you remind a child to say please, do so as part of good speech, not as a requirement for getting what he wants. Be sure he or she hears a lot of good speech from you. If you overemphasize politeness, you will teach your child to be a pushover.

Correct Politely: Have you ever wondered why some children are so polite and others are not? Children MUST experience a polite environment for them to be polite to others. The main reason is that they are brought up in an environment that expects good manners. One day, I noticed a family entering a hotel. The father looked at his two sons Ken and Ben, ages five and seven, and said, "Now, children, hold the door for your mother," which they did. I asked him why his children were so well mannered. He replied,"We expect it." As a parent, you have to expect appropriate behaviors from your child, coach those behaviors and supervise to ensure the learning is satisfactory.

instilling respect
a. Make it clear what respectful behavior is and what it is not, and insist that it (respectful behavior) be followed by all in the family, consistently.

b. Discuss the rules of respectful behavior with your child, taking into consideration his or her age.
c. Treat your child with respect. Do not allow yourself to get into an

argument with the child. If he or she happens to mess up, explain what exactly he or she has done wrong, the need to correct the mistake and why. Write a contract with your child, making sure the child is able to focus on one behavior at a time.

d. If your child behaves disrespectfully, let him or her experience the natural consequences of the behavior.

e. Reward/reinforce your child when he or she changes to respectful behavior.

f. Encourage your child to ask for permission and/or discuss things he or she wants to do in advance to avoid misunderstandings and increase the likelihood of finding solutions to disagreements without acting disrespectfully.

g. Encourage your child to express feelings and teach him/her how to talk about feelings in a controlled manner.

h. Be a good role model on respectful behaviors.

i. Record your child when behaving disrespectfully to let him or her hear or view himself or herself.

j. Intervene earlywhen you find your child behaving disrespectfully, and do not allow him or her to return to the situation unless you are sure they are going to behave appropriately.

k. Make sure your child gets attention for behaving appropriately to satisfy his or her need for attention.

l. Reduce emphasis on the kind of competition that may lead to anger, frustration, embarrassment and the attendant emotional outbursts.

m. Increase your child's awareness of other people's feelings and the need for the feelings of other people to be respected without necessarily giving in to their wishes and directions.

Hilda's Case
Hilda, a three-year-old, loves to go to the altar to greet a senior clergy's wife. As she approaches the altar, she bows the way she sees priests do, then lifts her hand gently towards the senior clergy's wife and seeks for permission. When permission is granted, she happily heads towards the senior clergy's wife and says, "Mama mchungaji (pastor's wife), thank you for loving me." She sits on her lap for a little while and then says, "Mama mchunganji, God bless you." Any time she says that the senior clergy's wife sheds tears of approval for this little girl and tells her, "You will become a

great person in this world," Hilda smiles and goes away to look for her mother.

Little Hilda has not only learnt modesty and respect from clergy but from what her parents tell her. Her perspective of getting attention from other people is that she has to start by conveying reverence and then she can be accepted. She has also realized it gives her a payoff therefore, she will continue practicing it. Like the senior clergy's wife tells her, she will always be privileged in life because she has learnt how to endear herself to others.

Social Difficulties

This is inability to live with others in ways that promote unity and cohesion in a group or community. It makes an individual unable to cope in many social systems or setups. Your child will not learn coexistence naturally; only systematic training will assure you of that ability. Pro social behaviors helps a child meet his/her own needs and community needs via social life.

Instilling Social Behavior

a. Establish rules of interaction with others that are consistent and followed by all in the family.

b. Supervise the child as much as is necessary when he/she is interacting and reward him/her for the rules adhered to once the activity is over.

c. When the child is not interacting well, explain to him/her what he/she is not doing right and what should be done.

d. Write a contract with your child in an effort to deal with the inappropriate social behavior.

e. Intervene early when your child starts getting into socially unacceptable behavior.

f. Teach your child how to express feelings without hurting others.

g. Arrange for your child to be involved in many activities with other children in order to help him/her learn the skills necessary to interact appropriately with others.

h. Do not laugh at or ignore your child when he/ she makes social mistakes.

i. Discuss alternative behaviors with your child after he/ she makes a social mistake.

j. Let your child experience the natural consequences of social mistakes committed, and make him/ her aware of the existence of a direct connection between the mistakes and the consequences.

k. Notify the parents of your child's friends of your child's challenge so that they can increase supervision and help you with instilling the acceptable behaviors.

l. Teach your child the importance of relationships and how he/ she can be developed and nurtured.

m. Encourage your child to participate in supervised co-curricular activities at school or in other social settings, such as religious activities.

n. Help your child to appreciate the dangers of having friends with social difficulties.

o. Assess your child for any form of abuse on him/ her because this can cause social difficulties. If there are positive indications, refer the child to a child therapist for support.

dishonesty

This is the inability to acknowledge the truth and/or acting to conceal reality. Your child may learn to be dishonest so that he/she can avoid consequences of a behavior. You may even push your child to being untruthful if you do not reward honesty. Your child can earn a trip for becoming truthful over something that was painful to reveal.

Instilling Honesty

a. Establish rules of honesty that are to be followed consistently by all in the family. Keep reminding your children about the benefits of honesty.

b. Model honesty by accepting mistakes and the consequences. c. Supervise your child as much as necessary when he/she is interacting with others and reward him/her for honesty.

d. When your child is not honest, explore the threats that make him/her dishonest.

e. Deal with dishonesty directly through writing a contract with your child on being honest with you and others.

f. Allow natural consequences to occur when your child is dishonest and make them see a direct connection between the dishonesty and the consequences.

g. Promote an open and honest line of communication with your child that encourages truth.

h. Do not punish your child's genuine forgetfulness, accidents and being a victim of situations with inadequate evidence.

i. Make your child understand that dishonesty does not prevent consequences, and that it results in even more negative consequences.

j. Avoid making accusations that can make your child lie.

k. Do not make the punishment so severe to make your child lie to avoid the punishment.

l. Encourage your child to come to you when there is a problem to help him/her avoid lying. If he/she comes to you in advance, consider lifting possible consequences. It makes the child learn that though being honest is risky, it is rewarding and liberating.

m. Do not punish your child for every mistake he/she does, this would encourage dishonesty.

n. Notify teachers and other caregivers dealing with your child that he/she has a dishonesty problem and work out a plan with them to correct the behavior.

o. When your child behaves in dishonest ways, calmly confront him/ her with the truth. Do not make him/ her fearful of being honest.

p. Develop a system of shared responsibility. If you get things in a mess, you may involve everybody in clearing the mess instead of trying to figure out who is responsible.

Selfishness

This is the inability to share what one has with others, even when it is necessary that one does so. Such a child is egocentric, thus becoming over involved with self. The natural tendency of infants is being overdemanding while being insensitive to others. They are only able to connect with their needs but not other people's needs. They are not refusing to be sensitive but they are limited because of their age. You have to designate time within which you can teach selflessness.

Instilling Selflessness

a. Establish rules of sharing that are to be followed by all in the family consistently.

b. Supervise your child as much as possible when interacting with others and reward him or her for sharing.

c. When the child is selfish,explain to him/her what he/she is not doing right and what ought to be done.
d. Do not allow selfish behavior; encourage realistic giving that promotes coexistence.
e. Intervene earlywhen your child starts to exhibit selfish behavior.
f. Allow natural consequences to occur when your child is selfish for the child to see a direct connection between selfishness and the consequences.
g. Arrange for your child to be engaged in activities that require teamwork and sharing.
h. Have objects and materials that everyone can use.
i. Role model sharing for your child and discuss it with him or her.
j. Remember, not all possessions have to be shared; therefore, make a distinction between when a child is selfish and when he/she is marking appropriate boundaries in regard to what belongs to him or her and what should be given out. This helps the child balance self-love with love for others.
k. Make sure that things shared with others are returned.
l. Establish clear rules about giving and receiving.

lack of Self-Control

This is the inability to take charge of self. In children, it is manifested

through peer pressure and lack of assertiveness. Such a child may get under the control of his/her emotions,specific behaviors and obsessive thoughts and, as a result, disregard other more important issues.

Instilling Self-Control

a. Establish rules and regular routine, for instance a timetable of activities, for your child to follow.

b. Closely supervise the implementation to make sure activities are time bound concerning starting and finishing.
c. When the child successfully controls himself/herself, reward him/her.
d. Consider the child's age and make sure that he/she is paying attention when you give instructions. Keep reminding the child about the instructions.
e. The activities planned for a child should be for a measured period to take care of his/her limitations in concentration.
f. Engage your child in something interesting, and when it is time to stop,

give permission for stopping. When working alone, provide a time reminder and caution when it is not adhered to.

g. After you have said no to a behavior, give an alternative.

h. Teach your child how to express emotions in a socially acceptable manner.

i. On realizing that your child is overdoing something, intervene early enough to avoid guilt and frustration.

j. Do not unduly highlight your child's lack of control, since he/ she may take advantage of it to get attention.

k. Write a contract on self-control and model the habit for the child.

Teach your child problem-solving skills. These include, identifying the problem, setting goals and objectives, developing strategies and developing a plan of action. Make sure that the method is followed in dealing with his/her problems.

Being Defiant

Defiance means open refusal to obey and it can be very frustrating to a parent. You certainly feel disrespected and frustrated. Defiant behaviors may range from not taking no for an answer, doing things at one's chosen, not the required time, failing to cooperate and doing what one deems right.

Instilling Obedience

a. Establish rules regarding defiance,and have the rules followed by all in the family. The rules should be followed consistently and guardians should closely monitor adherence to them.

b. Demonstrate how to obey by giving the child directives and then following the directions with him/her.

c. Give instructions directly to the child and at close range. Also, seek to know whether he/she has understood them.

d. Teach your child the value of compromise and obedience in order that both you and your child can be satisfied with outcomes.

e. When you tell your child what to do, be sure you explain the reason.

f. Make sure that your child understands the dangers of disobeying and doing what he/ she chooses.

g. Defiant children are self-directing but in deviant ways; let your child learn to be self-directing in enhancing ways.

h. Reduce chances of disobedience by discussing in advance and reaching agreements; and seek for alternatives.

Children should be helped to appreciate how obedience promotes favor amongst others, likeability, team work, cohesiveness, collaborative interactions and productivity.

management of finances
Handling money is an important aspect of life that children need to learn early enough while still living with parents. You should train your child on how to handle money so that the child can develop a healthy money management culture. Children who get a chance of learning how to handle money in their foundational years feel capable of dealing with their lives in adulthood.

Handling Money
a. Give your child chances to earn his/her own money. You can for example, give him/her an allowance for a job well done. Give him/her an opportunity to decide how to use the money he/she has earned, and let him/her use it with limited guidance.

b. Show your child your own good saving habits. Let him/her know when you achieve an objective. Share with him/her how long it took for you to achieve the objectives and the small steps you went through.

c. Play with him/her games that involve counting money and giving change.
d. Engage him/her in shopping and let him/her explain to you the amount of money he/she is carrying and the amount of change they are supposed to get back.
e. Give him/her opportunities to assist in raising money for projects in the community, school, religious institutions and for needy populations.
f. Teach your child the right attitude to money as a resource. Let him/her know that money is not everything in life and work. Integrity is far more important than money itself, though money can help in gaining integrity.
g. Teach him/her the value of money. Irrespective of the amount, any money has value and requires to be saved rather than being wasted.
h. Teach him/her that money is a product of hard work. Discuss with him/her about your work and the challenges you go through to earn money.

Influence of Mass Media

The influence of the media on the psychosocial development of your child is profound. As a parent, you should ensure age-appropriate use of all media, including television, radio, music, video games and the Internet.

Television Viewing

Television has the potential to generate both positive and negative effects, particularly on children and adolescents (Dietz & Strasburger, 1991; Johnson, Cohen, Smailes, Kasen & Brook, 2002). Your child's developmental level is a critical factor in determining whether the media will have positive or negative effects. Not all television programs are bad, but when your child is exposed to violence, inappropriate sexuality and offensive language, the impact is negative.Television viewing limits your child's time for vital activities such as playing, reading, learning to talk, spending time with peers and family, storytelling, participating in regular exercise, and developing other necessary physical, mental and social skills.

Keddy's Case

By the time Keddy completed her Fourth Form, her parents had started getting very worried about her lifestyle. She watched TV and videos almost the whole night and she hardly did any household chores. She had very conflictual relationships with her parents due to her nocturnal activities and hardly talked with her eldest sister. Over time, Keddy even became suicidal due to the emptiness she experienced. She was also having multiple sexual relationships,which she described as abusive.The material she watched encouraged her behaviors and though she had realized the harm she inflicted on herself, she had completely become hooked to the television. Keddy's parents knew they should have put restrictions on her regarding watching TV and playing video games but were now powerless.

Keddy had developed an addiction of watching TV and videos. This behavior had precluded other survival and gainful activities. She had picked other damaging behaviors like having unplanned sexual activities. This clearly demonstrates that she had lost love for herself and was incapable of self-control and self-care. It begs the questions, had she defined who she was and who she wanted to be? Does she understand what love for oneself means? Has she defined her values, principles and beliefs? The amount of time spent watching television and sitting in front of computers can affect a child's postural development. Excessive amounts of time at a computer can contribute to obesity, undeveloped social skills and a form of addictive behavior. Although rare, some children with seizure disorders are more prone to attacks triggered by a flickering television or computer screen.

Music Videos

Inappropriate music videos have a significant behavioral impact by glamourizing violence and making your teenager more likely to approve of premarital sex. In such videos, women, for example, are portrayed as arrogant, and this affects children's attitude towards certain gender. Attractive role models are portrayed as arrogant, naughty, aggressive and violent. Hence, music videos may reinforce false stereotypes in your child who may regard what they are watching as factual. Music lyrics have become increasingly explicit, particularly with reference to sex, drugs and violence. As a parent, you should take an active role in monitoring the music your child watches and listens to.

Video Games

Some video games may help in the development of fine motor skills and coordination of your child. However, you should discourage your child from playing violent video games because they can have harmful effects on his/her mental development (Dietz & Strasburger, 1991). You should familiarize yourself with various rating systems for video games and use this knowledge to make helpful decisions. The effect of violent video games on children is a real concern and as a parent, you should vet the video games your child plays.

Internet

You may feel outsmarted or overwhelmed by your children's computer and Internet abilities, or fail to appreciate that new media is an essential component of the new literacy, in which your children need to be proficient in.However,feelings of inadequacyor confusion should not prevent you from intentionally seeking to discover the Internet's benefits. The dangers inherent in this relatively uncontrolled 'wired' world are many and varied, but often hidden. These dangers should be unmasked by immersing yourself in the medium and exploiting the advice from the many resources aimed at protecting children, while allowing them to reap the 'wired' world's rich benefits in a safe environment. If you feel challenged as a parent, seek support from a life coach, internet savvy individuals, a counsellor or psychologist who is well versed with the effects of this medium.

The Internet has significant potential for providing children and the youth with access to educational information and can be compared to a huge home library. However, the lack of editorial standards limits the Internet's credibility as a source of information. There are other concerns as well; these include pedophiles who use the Internet to lure young people into relationships. There is also the potential for children to be exposed to pornographic material. As a parent, you can use technology that blocks access to pornography and sex talk on the Internet, but must be aware that this technology does not replace the children's need for parental supervision or guidance. Children are naturally curious; they will therefore want to find out information about diverse subjects. As a parent, you can manage this curiosity by as much as possible educating your child about various subjects. This can reduce the need to secretly browse the internet to find answers especially for subjects that require guidance such as sex and drugs.

Media Impact on Children's Behavioral Tendencies
Children are like a sponge that sucks any liquid poured on it. What they watch and hear becomes imprinted in their minds. The media is like a teacher who instills knowledge, attitudes, values and behavioral tendencies in children. The following are behavioral tendencies imprinted in children by the media, violence, poor nutrition, sexual promiscuity, drinking alcohol and smoking. These are presented as cool behaviors for celebrities. I will examine these dangers more exhaustively here after:

Violence
Violence on television is on the rise. The following groups of children may be more vulnerable to violence on television:

a. Emotionally disturbed children
b. Children with learning disabilities
c. Children who are abused by their parents
d. Children living in distressed families

Such children learn that violence is a way of handling conflicts and emotional issues.

Nutrition

Television takes time away from play and other such activities that help exercise young people, hence children who watch a lot of television are less physically fit and more likely to eat high fat and high energy snacks. The number of hours of television viewing corresponds to the risk of cholesterol levels in children (Dietz & Strasburger, 1991). Television can also contribute to eating disorders in teenage girls, who may emulate the slim role models seen on television. Eating meals while watching television should be discouraged because it may lead to less meaningful communication and arguably, poor eating habits.

Sexuality

Today, television has become a leading sex educator in Kenya. Most stations expose children to adult sexual behaviors in ways that portray irresponsible relationships, as normal and risk-free, "Everybody does it" seems to be the slogan. Statistics show that sex between unmarried partners is shown 24 times more often than sex between spouses, while sexually transmitted infections and unwanted pregnancies are rarely mentioned (Resnick et al.,1997).Some people and organizations believe that the media can influence sexual responsibility by promoting birth control methods, such as condom use, but mention of the emotional problems that go with such lifestyles is conveniently avoided.

Alcohol and Smoking

Television advertising glamorizes smoking and drinking of alcohol.

But while television is not the only way by which children learn about the use of tobacco and alcohol, concern arises from the fact that the consequences of these behaviors are not accurately depicted in this medium of communication.

Commercials can have profound effect on the developmental stage of your child. Young children do not understand the hidden dangers of TV commercials; they believe everything they are told and may even assume theyare being deprived of what could give them manybenefits. Yet this is because young children do not understand the difference between a program designed to entertain and a commercial designed to sell.

recommendations
a. You should intentionally explore the media with your child and discuss their educational value.

b. You should encourage your child to objectively analyze and critique what he/she sees in the media. You can also help children differentiate between fantasy and reality, particularly when it comes to sex and violence as portrayed in the media.

c. You should not allow your child to have a television, computer or video game equipment in his or her bedroom. For ease of monitoring his/her use, you should put these gadgets in a central location where they can be easily accessed and passwords known to all.

d. Television watching should be limited to less than 2 hours per day. You may want to consider more creative and interactive ways to spend time together.

e. You should offer your older child an opportunity to make choices by planning the week's viewing schedule in advance. Ideally, you should supervise these choices and be good role models by making wise choices concerning what they view.

f. You should explain why some programs are not suitable and praise your child for making good and appropriate choices.
g. You should limit the use of television, computers or video games as a diversion or substitute teacher.
h. You should ask alternative caregivers to maintain the same rules for media use in your absence.

rules as a Strategy of Correcting Behavior
Children having behavioral problems lack in basic skills of fitting in a

social context. It causes disharmony and social disorder and exposes the child to negative consequences. Rules are inevitable in determining boundaries for your child. When your child grows older, you should involve him/her in determining the kind of rules that regulate his/her behavior and healthy lifestyle. Doing the following will be helpful:

a. Establish rules pertaining to different aspects of life. They should be consistently followed by everyone at home. Discuss the rules often. Make your child tell you the expected rules before engaging in an activity where the rules are expected to apply. Before engaging the child in something, review the rule guiding the activity.

b. Supervise the child as much as is necessary and reward him or her for the rules adhered to once the activity is over.
c. If the child acts inappropriately, explain to him/her what exactly they have done wrong. Correct him/her as quickly as possible, reminding him/ her of the rule broken and what was expected.
d. Model for the child adherence to rules. Make sure that you follow the rules.
e. In cases where the rule may not apply, make the child understand.
f. Let the child experience the natural consequences of breaking the rule.
g. Avoid positive reinforcement for negative behavior by smiling, laughing or giving such positive responses when a rule is broken.

Parental involvement in Children's well-Being

Your child will attain healthy development when you are positively involved in his/her life. This means you provide for him/her, show open interest in meeting his/her needs, engage in play with him/her, coach certain skills and follow through with regular supervision. This involvement communicates support and interest for your child and it makes him/her feel secure and accepted. Such involvement has positive impact in the following:

a. Emotional fitness: When you are there for your child as he/she goes to bed, wakes up, and comes home from school, he/she grows in emotional well-being than a child whose parents are absent. In my counselling with children, they have reported that they feel safe and peaceful when their parents are available and they are able to concentrate on core businesses of their life.

b. Self-worth: When you are affectionate with your child and you are responsive to his/her needs, he/she regards him/herself as worthy. Your child does not feel lost in this dynamic world, but he/she feels there is a present coach and mentor who celebrates him/her.

c. Educational Prowess: When you are present for your child, to provide, guide and instruct, your child feels more assured and certain about progress. They even perform better when you are behaving responsibly to emerging issues in your life. He/she is able to trust and believe that no matter what happens, you will care, protect and nurture. This makes your child focus his/her energies on meaningful achievement.

d. Behavior: When you are available for your child to assess, guide and coach on desirable behaviors, your child is able to acquire age appropriate behaviors. This makes him/her feel adequate. This continuous interest and commitment to your child helps you pick behaviors that have to be worked on. In my counselling, I have observed such children rarely sink into, anxieties, conduct disorders, panic disorders and depression.

e. delinquency: I have repeatedly noted from children and adolescents I have worked with that they are hardly reactive through rebelliousness and abrasiveness if their parents are affectionate, supportive and responsive to their needs. It is also noteworthy from my clinical work that children also thrive best if their parents' marriage is harmonious and if both parents exert concerted effort in dealing with family affairs. Your child is even more ordered if you are deliberate and careful to parent skillfully. If you are responsibly honest with your child as a single parent regarding the absence of the other parent, you boost wellness in your child and hence he/she will have no need to engage in delinquent behaviors.

g. Sexual Behavior: When you teach values and beliefs to your child during the formative stages, you put a foundation of healthy sexual life. You should instill in your child right and wrong sexual beliefs, values and behaviors.

Ingrind's Case
Ingrind was told by her mother when she was thirteen years that when she has sex, she needs to be careful to use a condom so that she does not get pregnant. From this teaching, she understood her mother was giving her a

go-ahead to have sex as long as she used protective measures. Now, Ingrid is a sex addict and she is finding it very difficult to recover from it. Any time she tries to refrain, she gets depressed and she has to go back to having sex again with multiple partners to be mentally sober.

h. Teen Pregnancy: I have noted from children I have worked with in counselling that a parent's absence in their children's life can increase the likelihood of such children child having unplanned pregnancy. Hence, your absence may make your child feel neglected and hence look for love from other people. Additionally, teenage girls whose fathers are absent in their life tend to look for love from men; in their own words, to compensate for love they did not get from their biological fathers.

i. alcohol, Cigarettes and drug use: When you are available, responsive and supportive of your child, this becomes a protective factor to your child engaging in alcohol, cigarettes and drug use. Having a healthy attachment with your child shields him/her from engaging in psychoactive substances. Again, if you do not model alcohol, cigarettes and drug use, your child will hardly adapt into that behavior. If you model negative attitudes to psychoactive substances use, your child takes that as a standard to emulate. Unfortunately, parents in the 21st century are not sacrificial for their children. Many parents feel they will miss out in action if they do not gratify their desires and that is where we go wrong. Many parents who have taken that stance have lived to regret their choices when they watch helplessly as their children get ruined by addictive lifestyles that they modeled. One parent once said, "Who says I should not keep wines in our fridge? I will forbid our children never to indulge in beers and wines until they are of age." This is the attitude of most 21st century parents, they do not deny themselves for the sake of their children. They inculcate favorable attitudes towards drugs and alcohol by their liberal behaviors.

managing Sibling rivalry

Siblings are children of the same parents while rivalry is conflicting and competing riskily with each other or not agreeing on crucial issues. Conflicts and disagreements amongst any social unit are normal, siblings not excepted. There are many situations that can promote sibling rivalry and as a parent, you need to understand the sources of your children's rivalry so that you can deal with it successfully. Some of the prevalent sources include:

a. You maybe casual and not teach and coach unity and cohesion for harmonious relating of your children and therefore allow conflicts to simmer and escalate

b. You may not be committed to resolving emerging sibling rivalry c. Feelings of anger, self-pity and resentment due to perceived comparison with other siblings negatively. This may be due to a sibling performing comparatively better than another sibling does. If this is not handled well with due respect to every child it can precipitate to fights and conflicts

d. Feeling unloved and underprivileged compared to other siblings
e. Fear of being displaced and abandoned
f. Competition over resources, that is, who does what and who gets what
g. Unresolved conflicts
h. Having different interests because of being at different ages
i. Your children, boys and girls may have value differences that make them disagree
j. Your children may have different personalities and temperaments thus making them have different ways of viewing and responding to situations. This may make them develop conflicts and differences that maybe irreconcilable.
k. You may not have prepared your child about a pregnancy. When the child is born, the older child may feel threatened that his/ her space and what he/she enjoyed maybe taken away. Resolving sibling rivalry does not mean treating your children equally. It is simply not possible; it is difficult to accord equal treatment to all your children. When Purity has a birthday or is ill, she is the one who merits the special attention and presents.

Paul's Case
I taught Paul in high school and one day when he was in form two, he followed me as I went out of class. In class, I had signed off the lesson by talking about the adverse effects of using psychoactive drugs. Outside, he told me, "Teacher, I want to stop using drugs because they have started endangering my life." "What has made you think about changing?" I asked. Paul replied, "Last holidays we went to the joint where we buy drugs, there

*was a fracas and my friend was killed. I am so frightened and I fear I will
also lose my young life. I have never seen death so close." I asked him,"What
made you start using drugs in the first place?" He answered, "My mother did
not tell me there was a child on the way, and I just saw mum come with a
baby one evening. I have never loved my brother, I beat him up and I am so
aggressive with him. I have caused him so much pain. I wish my mum
prepared me for his coming, I think I just needed reassurance that I was still
important even if there was a new born child. I will apologize for all the
harm I have done to my innocent, young brother."*

Ways of handling sibling rivalry

a. Do not make comparisons. A parent may say to her second born child
Mike, *"When your sister Pascalina was your age she could tie her shoe
laces."* Mike maybe a little slower in learning the skill of tying shoe laces but
that does not mean he is abnormal. He may require more coaching but not
being told he is inadequate.

b. Do not dismiss or suppress your children's resentment or angry feelings.
Contrary to what many people think, anger is not something we should try to
avoid at all costs. It is an entirely normal part of being human, and it is
certainly normal for siblings to get furious with one another. They need the
adults in their lives to help them resolve their differences amicably.

c. Understand the source of conflicts, for example, when a child claims not to
be loved, listen without being defensive, if it's true your action seems like
favoritism, assure your child you are going to be more considerate of
him/her. If the child is unrealistic, help the child examine his/her reasoning so
that he/she can arrive at a more objective way of looking at the situation.

d. When possible, let brothers and sisters settle their own differences. Then
be alert so that you can know when it is time to step in and mediate,
especially in a contest of unequals in terms of strength, talents, personality,
age, gender, eloquence etc.

e. Introducing a newborn child to the others and helping them appreciate, all
of them are important and they have a place in your family.

f. Coach your children on skills of dealing with one's negative feelings and facilitating harmony. You should take your children through role-plays so that they can master the art of reconciliation. These may include:

• Admitting to having a negative feeling
• Understanding the communication that the negative feeling is making. For example, anger may mean a child is feeling unfairly treated
• Check whether the feeling is unrealistic
• Confront the feeling and deal with the issue rationally. For example, "I feel hurt when you call me foolish, because I know I am not foolish. Moreover, you are my sibling and you should address me with respect."

Parental monitoring and Supervision

Every parent longs for a well-disciplined, emotionally balanced, socially skilled child who is excelling in all aspects of life. Parental monitoring facilitates the delivery of the brand a parent would want his or her child to be. Parental monitoring includes:

i. The expectations you have of your child's behavior ii. The actions you take to keep track of your child's behavior iii. The ways you respond when your child or teenager breaks the

rules. You are exercising parental monitoring when you ask your child or teen: Where will you be? Whom will you be with? When will you be home?

Monitoring should start during early childhood and continue throughout the teen years, evolving, as the child grows older. As children develop into teenagers, adults might view them as more independent and less in need of monitoring. However, consistent monitoring throughout the teen years is critical. The teens' desire for independence can bring opportunities for unhealthy or unsafe behaviors. Nevertheless, what can the parents do to monitor their teens effectively? The following are some steps you can take to monitor your teen and help protect him or her from risky behaviors:

a. Talk with your child or teen about your rules and expectations, and explain the consequences for breaking the rules.
b. Talk and listen to your child or teen often about how he/ she feels and what he/she is thinking.

c. Know who your child or teen's friends are.
d. Talk with your child or teen about the plans he/she has with friends, what he/she is doing after school, and where he/she will be going.
e. Set expectations concerning when your child or teen will come home, and expect a call if he/she is going to be late.
f. Ask whether an adult will be present when your child or teen is visiting a friend's home.
g. Get to know your child or teen's boyfriend or girlfriend. h. Get to know the parents of your child or teen's friends.
i. Talk with your relatives, neighbors, your child or teen's teachers, and other adults who know your child or teen. Ask them to share what they observe about your child or teen's behaviors, moods, or friends.
j. Watch how your child or teen spends money.
k. Keep track of how your child or teen spends time online, and talk about using Internet safely.
l. Pay attention to your child or teen's mood and behavior at home, and discuss any concerns you might have.
m. If your child or teen does break a rule, enforce the consequences fairly and consistently.
n. Make sure your child or teen knows how to contact you at all times.

What Children Need

Children need acceptance
They need praise and appreciation
They need to learn they can trust their parents not to deceive them or break their promises
They need consistency and fairness
They need to feel their fears, feelings, their inexplicable impulses, their frustrations and their inabilities are understood by their parents They need to know exactly where their limits are, what is permitted and what is prohibited
They need to know that their home is a safe place, a place of refuge, a place where they have no need to be afraid
They need positive spiritual leadership, example and encouragement They need warm approval when they do well and firm correction when they do wrong
They need to learn a sense of proportion
They need to know their parents are stronger than they are, are able to

weather the storms and dangers of the outer world and also able to stand up to their children's rages and unreasonable demands They need to feel their parents like them and can take time to listen They need perceptive responses to their growing need for independence

Author Unknown

Chapter 8

ChaPTEr EighT
ShaPiNg yOur Child'S malENESS aNd fEmalENESS

Every society which has tried to engineer sexual symmetry and destroy gender role differences has failed.
melanie Phillips

gender is the first form of identity

Etching natural tendencies of femaleness in a girl and maleness in a boy child insures them from a lifetime of identity crisis, confusion, fragmentation, indifference and self-justification. The physiological makeup, brain wiring and biochemistry of females differ dramatically from that of males. This makes boys and girls to think, feel and act differently to life's situations. When a child is born, he/she has an inbuilt expectation and orientation of needing love,attention,celebration, nurture, nourishment, protection, positive direction and guidance. When this lacks, the child develops deep-set resentment, aggression, anger, fragmentation, inconsistencies, antisocial behaviors, criminality and rebelliousness. The deficiencies a child experiences makes him/ her gravitate towards a negative route. In the same way, when a child's natural gender tendencies are not nurtured and established adequately, gender inconsistencies and conflicts develop that harass and disturb the individual throughout his/her lifespan.

When a child is born, the genitalia determine whether the child is referred to as a boy or a girl. Naming then follows, and there are unique names for boys and girls. Being referred to as a boy or a girl makes a child start developing gender compatible behaviors. The child starts discriminating what is appropriate or not appropriate to do or allow. Gender identity refers to attaining values, attitudes and behaviors congruent to one's gender.

Transgender refers to the development of a gender identity, which is discordant with the gender of rearing and genital anatomy. In situations where hormones, genetic makeup and anatomical composition predisposes a child to gender conflicts, comprehensive assessment should be carried out by a team of relevant professionals (medics, psychologists, counsellors, sociologists, neurosurgeons) which would inform diagnosis and possible interventions. When such cases are handled with care and precision, informed and accountable handling of such cases is initiated so that the child can be saved from a lifetime of perpetual conflicts and unending emotional issues. An improper and uninformed parental response to gender inconsistencies is grossly harmful to children, and should be avoided at all costs since it affects the way a child views self, the world and all aspects of life. You possibly do not want to set your child up to be a failure in life; unable to respond realistically to a multifaceted life.

To shape maleness and femaleness, the parent must be aware of each gender's natural needs. In traditional African communities, each gender was given gender appropriate chores and tasks. Values were ingrained and children were assigned mentors. Training one to be a girl or a boy was a community obligation and community elders were concerned with preserving their community through developing healthy men and women.

In the 21st century, parenting is an individual parent's responsibility and therefore a very daunting task. The bio-psycho-social aspects of both boys and girls place different demands on parenting each gender. Parents should appreciate that in shaping the gender of each child, they are grounding them to be successful as people in their marriages and families. Many people whose gender and sex identities are not clearly defined are predisposed to depression and other mental disorders due to internal and external pressures and a deep sense of rejection and 'lostness.' Definition of oneself against one's anatomical gender naturally aligns with oneself and does not introduce conflicts that present identity crisis. Every child, male or female, requires appropriate self-definition. Genesis 5:2 says, *"He created them male and female and blessed them. And he named them "Mankind" when they were created."*

Girls require another loving nurturing woman to define, shape and celebrate their womanhood and femaleness. Likewise, boys require a nurturing, steadfast and caring man to define, shape and celebrate their manhood and manliness. In the absence of same gender nurturer, a suitable loving mentor should be found to instill and fortify the fundamentals of manhood and womanhood. Such mentors can have timelines and articulate essential values, beliefs, worldviews, abilities and capacities that require ingraining for manliness and womanliness to be developed. Mentoring, coaching, instructing, guiding, directing, training and systematically monitoring learning are key essentials in molding an all-rounded man or woman.

Parental supervision is quite an integral task in the development of maleness and femaleness. Supervision picks on developmental tasks, strengths and challenges in each child and relevant interventions are crafted. Parental supervision identifies when a child is having gender developmental challenges and lays a foundation on which gender identityformation is facilitated.Parental supervision entails affirmation of maleness and femaleness for the child to attain confidence in either being male or female. For example, when a boy breaks his voice, the parents should communicate to him that that is a sign of maleness. When children are comfortable with their own gender, they are able to move on and deal with other developmental tasks.

Marvin's Case
Marvin was a second born in his family. He was ten years when his desire to be a girl became apparent. He would take his older sister's clothes, wear them, and feel good. The foster parent used to find that weird and one time she disclosed this to a pastor who advised her to take him to church for prayers. Marvin's mother had left for Dubai when he was two years old and Marvin hardly knew her but had deep-set longings for her. The pastor suggested that he should start attending catechism classes for his baptism so that correct moral and gender values and disciplines could be instilled. Marvin's desire to be a girl abated for a while until he reached form two when he started having vivid dreams of being a girl.

While in form three, he met another boy who was struggling with his gender identity and they decided to be expressive about their feelings and thoughts. The other boys branded them "crazy fellows" and there were many stories told about them. Marvin did not care what was said about him since he still excelled when it came to exams and sports. After his fourth form, he approached a doctor to help him transform to a girl. He even started calling himself Marlin. The aunt was beside herself with sadness and she summoned Marvin's mother to come home and deal with the issue.

Marvin's story conveys the complex nature of gender identity predicament.Marvin has plentiful internal conflicts that he is contending with and the aunt and pastor do not know what to do to help Marvin define himself appropriately. He does not have many friends in school because they consider him queer.

gender Stereotypes

The 21stcentury definition of feminine and masculine behaviors and characteristics is different from the traditional one. In the past, girls were only allowed to do feminine things like playing with dolls, cooking, collecting firewood, doing home chores and taking care of babies. They were expected to be more passive while today it is trendy for a girl to be aggressive and multi-skilled. Boys were expected to be more aggressive, unfeeling and to only show masculine behaviors. Boys who showed emotions and loved to be in the house were taunted and teased. Our expectations of "what girls are expected to do" and "what boys are expected to do" have changed dramatically. Today, girls frequently excel at sports and school subjects traditionally thought of as masculine. These include Chemistry, Physics and Biology. Boys too frequently excel in artistic subjects traditionally thought of as feminine like Christian education, Literature in English, Geography and History. Every child should be encouraged to undertake subjects, courses and careers they feel passionate about.

When a child's interests and abilities are different from what society expects, he/she is often subjected to discrimination and bullying. Think about a girl who chooses to pursue mechanical engineering, her preference maybe frowned at and this may affect the way she looks at herself. It is natural for parents to want their children to be accepted socially. However, children need to feel comfortable with their choices even if what they do is different from societal expectations. If your son does not excel in sports or even have an interest in them, for example, there will still be many other opportunities and areas in which he can excel. Not excelling in areas "he or she should" excel in does not make your child less masculine or feminine. Each child has his/her own strengths, and at times, they may not conform to society's or your own expectations, but they will still be a source of his/her current and future success. Keep encouraging these natural inclinations without assigning them to femaleness or maleness.

Finally, as a parent, you should not try to make your child fit in a prescribed way of doing things or even some particular preferences that do not resonate with his/her natural leanings. Allow your child to feel accepted with choices he/she makes regarding his/her career. Your concern should be, whatever your son or daughter choses to do, is he comfortable with his maleness and she with her femaleness. Does he celebrate his maleness and she her femaleness? That is the gist of the matter.

differences between Boys and girls

Boys Girls

Robust, physical, and forceful Relational, less abrasive, more reconciliatory
Use more physical aggression Use more verbal aggression

Naturally carefree and can subject themselves to harm when growing up because they are quick to act. Boys need to be reminded that there are times and places, like the classroom or indoor spaces, where they need to shift to a lower gear
Cautious and will often not rush to engage in activities. E.g. girls prefer to play around the compound as opposed to boys who often want to wander further from their home

Boys naturally bend forward in relationships and are territorial; they protect and defend their interests aggressively. E.g. they do not like the idea of another man showing interest in their girlfriend. They can also demonstrate compulsivity in relationships, which means you have to guide on healthy and unhealthy relationships.
Girls mostly bend backwards in relationships and expect boys to initiate relationships with them, defend and protect them. They can easily get depressed when they perceive rejection and as a parent, you have to guide on handling rejection and disappointments

Mature more slowly, particularly when it comes to language development, social skills and fine motor skills. On the other hand, boys' gross motor skills (running, jumping, and balancing) tend to develop slightly faster (Payne & Isaacs, 2002). Gross motor skills are movements that involve using the large muscles of the body
They develop their language, social and fine motor skills more rapidly than boys. Hence, they find it easy to learn household chores such as cleaning, cooking, sewing, plaiting etc

Think more than feel. Boys are more in touch with their thoughts than feelings; you have to help them access their feelings so that they can respond to situations more logically. This is something you can focus on when reading books with boys; point out characters' emotions, so boys start to notice how others are feeling

Girls naturally feel more
than think and are better at reading nonverbal signs, like tone of voice and expression, which also makes them better communicators early on, as they can connect feelings and words faster

raising Boys

As parents of boys, you are bringing up men who will be boyfriends, husbands, fathers, coworkers, bosses, professionals or presidents. Be careful, therefore, to teach your boy child to be strong and powerful, yet sensitive and understanding. You want your boy child to bring out his positive maleness in all situations of life and to celebrate his manliness in all those situations.Every parent will want to give each child the same opportunities, but it is worth knowing about the particular pressures and challenges girls and boys can face so you can work out the best ways to help them achieve their full potential. When you understand the difference between genders, your discipline, confidence-building and communication strategies have greater impact, particularly when parenting boys. Even though their brains are incredibly similar at birth, at the age of two when they first realize they are a boy or a girl, it can be a different story (Svare 1983).

While counselling boys together with their fathers, I have noted many fathers are pushy when dealing with their male children, sometimes too highhanded yet tender with their female children. By doing this, the male children feel rejected and disregarded.Fathers should be firm with their male children but also loving and nurturing in word and action. Since boys can be more chaotic and destructive than their sisters, fathers should coach more than being punitive. They should coach processes (like how you become an entrepreneur, how you develop leadership skills and how you provide protection and leadership), skills and competences required. Fathers should be good role models to their sons regarding strengths and attributes they want ingrained in them. Consequently, fathers should father themselves before fathering their sons.They should try to create a relationship with their sons; this makes the young boys have confidence in their male parents as coaches and mentors, not rivals. Where there is rivalry between sons and fathers, damage happens to the sons.

Dickson's Case
Dickson had attended three high schools because of suspensions. In the two schools before he was admitted to a third one, he had been caught selling drugs and having romantic relationships with other boys. From the sale of heroin and cocaine during the holidays, he could get more than two hundred thousand shillings, but it did not give him happiness. He also did not do much with that money since he wasted it in extravagant living. It was eminent the dad was too harsh on him, sometimes even violent with him. He had beaten him several times and once, before he was suspended from the second high school, the principal with great dismay saw the father pushing the boy into

the trunk of his vehicle. He had twice jumped out of his father's moving vehicle.

In a counselling session with Dickson and his dad,Dickson could not find words because in his own admission, he did not know what to talk about with his father since he was an enemy. He felt his father loved his younger brother not him. The father admitted he was too harsh with Dickson but because the boy deserved it.

Boys like Dickson display aggression, resentment and stubbornness because they feel hated, unwanted and a liability. Like Dickson's father, many male parents feel strongly that their boy children invite the treatment they receive from them. However, the behaviors displayed by their sons are a way of looking for attention, appreciation and consideration, but this signal is not understood by their dads. Dickson's father is too high handed and should moderate his way of dealing with his son. If he does not he may lose him to drugs, reckless living, suicide or other social ills. Dickson required more understanding, firmness and coaching on coexistence and sensitivity. To rear a boy adequately, parents should cultivate patience and appreciation of small steps made since boys are not obviously agreeable and loyal as girls.

Parenting Teenage Boys

Teenage boys need clear structures. As a parent, you need to know where he is and what he is doing at all times. Do not fall into the "You do not trust me"trap.The issue is not trust but a realistic assessment of the dangerous world that adolescents must negotiate. Before eighteen years, the teenager has not developed his cognition to be able to have clear judgment of issues and situations. Still teenagers are not able to perceive possible consequences of behavior because they are compulsive though they have a great need for independence.

Kilpatrick's Case

Kilpatrick was the only boy in a family of three children. The parents felt extraordinarily blessed to have a boy. He was a trusted, well-behaved boy in primary and secondary school. His sisters too were admired for their modesty and respect. When his parents visited him in school, teachers complimented them for being so successful in parenting. They in turn used to tell other parents how thankful they were, that their parenting investment had become so fulfilling.In form four,Kilpatrick started telling his parents that everyone wanted to control him and that he had never learnt to be his own person. Concerning that, he faulted his dad for wanting him to do only what he wanted. One evening when the family had gone out for an outing, he tearfully told his parents, "If ever I got married, I would not want to give birth to a baby boy because I would not know how to take care of him. You have taught me boys are not worth listening to, and anything they propose should be opposed vehemently." Then he turned to his dad and said, "I hate you dad for being too cruel and highhanded with me and not your girls." Kilpatrick is now in college and has been going home drunk and the parents are lost for words.

Younger boys can be a joy to parents when they are obedient, loyal and respectful. However, Like Kilpatrick, when they reach adolescence, they are more buoyant, aggressive and daring as they chart their own paths and look for ways of gratifying themselves. Hence, when your boy child enters adolescence, he needs to be parented differently. The testosterone surges that boys experience blunt their fear while making them prone to dangerous behaviors that both provoke and result in anger (Monaghan & Glickman, 1992).

Raising a Boy as a Single Mother
While raising a girl has its own challenges, raising a boy is especially

challenging because for them, so much of the growing up process revolves around their father. The man figure in the boy's life helps him learn how men think, express their feelings and behave. The most important rule to remember is that your boy needs both male and female role models. As a single mother, you provide the female nurturance, which includes understanding, providing help on a moment-tomoment basis, being available in times of need and providing affection. However, boys must have male examples, too, if they are to develop a healthy sense of self-esteem that will ensure their success when they reach adulthood. A strong, male role model helps the boy develop his strengths and talents, teach them about healthy competition,firmness and resilience,and help instill the confidence to help him/her meet the challenges of adulthood. The male role model helps the growing young man celebrate his maleness and discharge roles and responsibilities that enhance his maleness.

The most obvious solution for you as a single mother parenting a boy is to provide different, loving, male mentors to coach on different aspects of life like leadership, courage, responsibility, maleness, resilience and responsible risk taking. However, of those mentors, there should be one or two who are consistent to provide steadiness, mature attachment and stability, which are important aspects of life. If the boy's father loves him and is available, make sure they have a chance to spend quality time together, even if your own relationship with his father is imperfect. If he is not there, find other role models from within the family, religious institutions and from your circle of friends. This is particularly important as your boy approaches puberty, a time of considerable confusion and change. Nonetheless, it is important to appreciate that men also struggle with parenting male children, so being parented by a father is not a magic wand for healthy growth. Maybe the most important thing for a single mother to remember in raising a boy is that he needs a lot of extra love. You should look for reliable, caring mentors who will instill wholeness in the boy. If this is not provided, they live their lives feeling hopeless and incomplete, something that should be avoided at all costs. A boy needs from you as the mother to provide survival needs (nourishment, shelter and food), love and belonging (family and loved ones), fun (enjoyment and pleasure), freedom (responsible independence and autonomy) and power and esteem (recognition and celebrating his achievements).

Moreover, provide affirmation for your boy child; this teaches him to love himself. Go to his sports events and include yourself in his activities as much as you can. Tell him things like, "You make me so proud, you are going to be very successful in future, you provide us with security and protection the same way you will do to your future wife and children, your wife will be happy to have a responsible, confident, understanding and loving husband, you are an outstanding young man."These messages will instill in your boy a sense of confidence and pride, feelings that can be put at risk in the absence of a caring father. These statements will mainstream a sense of focus, confidence and pride in your son so that he does not see himself as missing in action as a man. He will know he was not parented by a father but he is not less of a man.

The Story of Dr. James Mwangi
Dr. James Mwangi is the current Group Managing Director and Group Chief Executive Officer of the Equity Group Holdings Limited. He gave an account of his mother, who had been widowed early in life, and had to singlehandedly look for ways and means to feed and raise him and his siblings in a deeply rural setting. He believes he owes his internationally recognized entrepreneurial success to his mother, who always told him he would be a great achiever in life. Dr. Mwangi once said,"There was no time for childish games; everyone had to chip in to keep things in the home running." Like the rest of his siblings, Dr. Mwangi had to do his share of chores. These included looking after livestock, making charcoal; selling fruits and other farm produce for small margins. He added, "Here was a woman well past the first flush of youth straining every sinew and using all her ingenuity not only to feed and clothe her children but was also determined that they go to school and learn."

The storyof Dr.James Mwangi,confirms that when a single mother is in tune with her boy children,making them celebrate their resourcefulness, talents, abilities and selfness, they grow up as exceptional males. Here was a child whose father was absent and did not play a central role in parenting this magnanimous guru. Nonetheless, the no-nonsense protective mother guaranteed they could eke out life for themselves in the midst of grievous challenges. As a single parent, you MUST make certain like Mwangi's mother that the boy child's core needs are met (survival, developmental, intellectual, emotional, spiritual, vocational and social).

Advice on Parenting Boys
Set Limits and Boundaries: Since boys can be very active, naughty and easily excitable, you should help them respect limits and boundaries.

Help Boys to Self-regulate: Boys generally are more impulsive than girls are, hence,you should help them to stop, reflect and act.

Model Good Behavior: Even when you are stressed about your son's boisterous, aggressive behavior, it is important to keep calm. You should understand that boys are physiologically different from girls and therefore exercise moderation in the way you discipline and punish him. Always spanking and shouting can heighten the impulsivity and feelings of being bad.

Ingrain Kindness and Sensitivity: Kindness and sensitivity do not come so naturally in your son. You have to teach them, supervise, appraise the level of learning and celebrate learnt lessons. Look for opportunities to develop positive, male role models that your son could emulate. Schedule time with dads, older brothers, uncles, and grandparents, or get involved in a volunteer mentoring program.

Provide Adequate Affection: Because of the aggressive and insensitive nature of boys when they are in their formative stages, it is natural to deny them affection while you may show open affection to your girl child. He too needs to have enough positive affection from you so that he does not go looking for love to fill in his hunger for it. When you communicate affection, your boy child will also easily give it out to other people.

Allow your Boy-child Freedom to be Himself: Remember that dirt washes off, but memories of fun play can last for years. So allow boys to play in the mud, but identify for them safe areas, whether in urban or rural areas. For fear of the noise, designate an area in your home. Play shapes a boy's temperament and personality.

Teach Responsibility: Since boys are not so tuned up for loyalty and being agreeable, they can seem rebellious and stubborn. Sometimes they would rather direct their sisters to do certain things rather than them doing those tasks. These may include cleaning his room, bathing, cleaning his clothes, cleaning the compound and feeding pets. Following directions and finishing tasks are skills that are often slowto develop in boys. Give appropriate responsibilities to aid in developing the skill, practice helps. A sense of responsibility will serve him well in school, and your home life will run more smoothly, too.

The key to teaching responsibility is to make sure your boy child understands this crucial fact; power, privilege, and responsibility go together. When responsibility is high, so are the other two and when it is low, so are the other two. Teenagers, especially boys, often feel powerless; they need to know that they have the power to affect what happens to them by behaving responsibly. They need to know in advance exactly how much power and privilege they will lose for specific irresponsible behaviors.

Help him Develop Social Skills: Girls form intimate relationships than boys, because they resonate with tenderness and care for others. Boys are more likely to play in groups and compete for leadership. Help your son develop stronger one-on-one friendships by encouraging him to share with others, use his good manners and generally play nice and firm.If you instill a strong sense of self in your son and encourage him to accept other people's differences, it will be easier for him to deal with any teasing that comes from being different.

Step up Praising and Celebrating your Boy-Child: "Boy" behavior, even when it is age-appropriate, can be hard for adults to deal with and boys, as a result, get plenty of correcting, reprimanding, and scolding in school and at home. However, you should be careful that you do not tell him off endlessly, particularly for things that happen outside his control in case he stops caring. Whenever possible, try to catch your son "being good." Let him know that you appreciate his efforts at selfcontrol and channel his energy into activities that are constructive and rewarding.

Let him Take Risks: Boys are risk takers because they are highly adventurous. Teach them on factoring consequences whenever they engage in activities. You can even supervise engagement in activities so that you can coach on responsible risk taking. Give them plenty of practice in risk assessment. Later on in life, they will plan for realistic risk engagements
Love your Son as he is: You may have wishes of the kind of a son you would have wanted to have but that is a fantasy.You have to be practical with who your male child is, and help him overcome challenges and deficiencies he may have. This means you have to refrain from comparing him with his sisters; he is just a different kind of breed that requires patience and latitude.

Help him Appreciate the Multifaceted Nature of Masculinity: Help your son appreciate the different aspects of masculinityand howhe can use them as strengths.These may include physical strength, exceptional mechanical abilities, rational at looking at situations and gifted in leadership.

Acknowledge Your Son's Feelings: In the African culture,boys are harassed when they express their emotions. Often times, they are shunned when they seek to be understood. When your son is moody and calling for attention verbally or non-verbally, he has a right to be heard so that he can resolve pent up emotions. You should not taunt him by telling him that he is he is not manly enough. Even men have feelings, which should be allowed and dealt with. That way, he feels accepted as a human being and he too can treat others in thoughtful ways.

Pick the Nonverbal Messages: Given that about seventy-five percent of communication is nonverbal; you have to tune yourself to picking, understanding and responding correctly to your son's nonverbal behaviors.

Action-Talk: Many boys talk more easily when they are moving and engaging in activity, so provide activities to help them express themselves.

Coach on Verbal and Physical Nonviolence: Let your son know that real manliness is not in verbally and physically violating others but in being understanding, ensuring inclusivity and firmness. Let him appreciate the gains of being manly but at the same time being considerate and sensitive.

Build Motivation in your Male Child: Open up conversations about motivation. Inculcate motivation in your son to accomplish tasks and celebrate him when he achieves to give it constancy. When your son achieves positive results after accomplishing a project, it will help him value motivation in every undertaking.

Train on Stress Management Skills: Help your son to use practical ways of dealing with stress.This mayinclude exploring the causes of stress,going for a retreat, engaging in physical exercises, participating in spiritual activities, giving services to community and engaging in meditation.

Lead by Example: Model to your son the behaviors and abilities which would make him a capable male. For example, you can model family leadership and responsibility through providing wise direction and initiating projects that are money generating. Explain to him the procedure so that he can have a clear mental map on how to counter certain situations.

Encourage Autonomy and Independence: Males yearn for autonomy and self-direction. Seek opportunities for training your son responsible independence. Help him grasp the essence of being accountable to other significant persons in his life.

Use Respectful and Positive Methods of Discipline: Lectures and punishments rarely work, at least not over the long haul, and they do not teach self-discipline.

Promote Safety Inside and Outside the Home: Demonstrate to your son the significance of guaranteeing safety when he is undertaking tasks. He should know safety comes first in any activity. Since it may not get easily ingrained in your boy child, continue with this lesson in all stages of his life until you determine the lesson has been learnt.

raising girls

You should ensure that your girl child is nurtured, protected, coached and provided with essential information and abilities at every developmental stage to help her surmount the emerging challenges and meet her developmental needs. Every child negotiates situations or a developmental stage at his/her own level of speed and precision. Respect her uniqueness and work with her at her level.

Girls are forced to start nurturing others when there is deficiencyin the care and protection of vulnerable members of the family. Unfortunately, when a child starts mothering others, she is denied an opportunity to receive care and protection herself, and her emotions get blunted, thus affecting her emotional health. Such girls can become self-destructive later on in life as they try to compensate for what they missed.

Chikisa's Case
Chikisa, a first-born in a family bedeviled by fights between her mother and father, now feels as if her life has slowly stopped. The most discerning child in the family, she remembers her mother lying on the floor during fights from when she was four years. She once told a friend she believed that her father had extra marital affairs but he always blamed it on her mother whom he suspected of being unfaithful. She understood his behavior to be a way of covering himself. From her early years, Chikisa had a compulsion for protecting her mother, and she often did so by insulting her dad and rebelling against him. Now, at 24 years, she has an anger problem, is addicted to spirits, has dropped out of college, is irresponsible, and steals from her mother or manipulates her so that she can get money for buying liquor. She says she is sad, hopeless, ugly, and has lost direction and the trust of her

family.

Chikisa is a caring perceptive girl, who relegated her developmental needs to take care of her purportedly vulnerable mother. As a young adult,she has become self-destructive and her family cannot understand her. She did not develop internal mechanisms of self-acceptance, self-reliance, resilience, good spiritedness, endurance and selfreconstruction. How did she miss this? Because her parents' marriage was rocky, they did not have the energies to parent sufficiently. She exemplifies a youngster who feels empty and lost in the adult world. She has to find herself,and input abilities,competences and rudiments to stabilize her and thrust her to another level.

Advice on Parenting Girls

The following is what you can do to build your daughter's confidence and resilience for the tricky years ahead:

Encourage Assertiveness: Girls can sometimes develop timidity, unable to stand up for themselves due to the innate tendency for relationships and being emotive. You should coach your daughter on self-awareness, self-resolve and assertiveness. She may be shy to say 'no' and feel ashamed of saying 'yes.' She should know she has a right to selfprotection even as she takes care of other people.

Help Her Overcome Self Pity: Girls love attention and approval.You should aid your daughter to feel capable and important in the presence of peers and friends. Assist her to deal with disappointment and rejection by coming out of those situations stronger and resilient.

Encourage a Healthy Body Image: Girls are evidently keen about their body image and negative feedback can be depressing. When she receives negative feedback from others, let her know she can come to you for comfort and reassurance. Make direct comments regarding her body image. You can tell her, "you are a very pretty woman," "you are graceful in the way you carry yourself," "you dress very modestly," or "you are a tidy young woman." These statements said genuinely will instill a sense goodness and self-appreciation.

Prepare her for Sexism: Sexism is gender-based prejudice or discrimination against girls and women based on their gender, cultural and societal attitudes, values, beliefs and stereotypes. Such may include "Men are stronger and more intelligent than women!" or "A woman's place is in the home, barefoot and pregnant! "Women cannot take elective positions in government and are poor leaders" or "Women are inferior to men and should be treated that way," or "the key role of a woman is to serve men." These stereotypes are not true and you should help your girl child to outgrow these labels so that she can enhance herself and stand out in areas she is talented in.

Suzanne's Case

When Suzanne joined university, she started working at modeling company, part time. She was increasingly conscious of her body image. She hardly had good appetite any more. She somehow feared that she would not look attractive if she ate more than she needed. After six months, her performance started declining, she started looking dull and depressed and she could vomit any time she ate. The university doctor diagnosed the condition as anorexia nervosa, a condition where an individual refuses to eat to be petite. Suzanne's friends and lecturers got concerned. She is now attending counselling sessions and she is starting to regain her composure and beauty.

Anorexia nervosa is a prevalent condition among young women who are overly keen about their body image. As a parent, you may feel helpless in the face of such a condition because you may not understand it well. Consult counsellors when there are behavioral tendencies you are not able to understand in your daughter. It is not weakness to ask what you are not clear about. Suzanne had taken beauty and good looks too far to a point of neglecting her health. She may not have looked at the implications of her tendencies and she needed her parents and others around her who were concerned to raise her awareness levels to what she was doing to herself.

Encourage Focused Motivation and Passion: Girls traditionally have always been looked at as push-overs. Placing your daughter second place would make her compare herself unfavorably to male siblings or the opposite gender. Let her know that whatever she sets her mind to pursue as long as it is gainful you will give it full support. She should know she has what it takes to excel in anyfield she is passionate about.

Strengthen Her Decision Making: In terms of gender prejudice, girls and women are not given enough liberty to make their own decisions.

Consequently, they develop a weak decision making mechanism, which becomes compromised when they have to make crucial decisions. You certainly want to develop your daughter to have confidence in decision-making. This means, you will allow her to make independent decisions and judgments though with supervision so that positive results are achieved. You should reduce your supervision as she grows, gets confident and is able to make constructive decisions.

Encourage Her to Take Physical Risks: When you tell your daughter, "these are boys' tasks," you make her shy away from taking on physical responsibilities. Let your daughter know it is okay to engage in physical tasks like riding a bicycle or a motor cycle or even repairing broken things. The more your daughter engages in such activities, the more she gets confident.These girls report an incredible sense of accomplishment and feeling of competence, both of which give a huge boost to self-esteem.

Communicate Unconditional Love: One thing that your daughter requires is confirmation that she is loved irrespective of her imperfections and limitations. It does not matter what her shortcomings are but it is important for you to communicate to her that she is admired and accepted not because of what she can achieve but for herself. She needs you to know the 'inner her' and validate the developing person within, as well as noticing her emerging young womanhood. *Listen to Her:* By being consistent, receptive and available to listen, you will eventually be let into her inner world. Let her use you as a sounding board to sort out what she is going through, without solving problems for her. The answers that come from within her are the ones she will eventually live by. When you listen to her in an understanding way, you help her attain self-discovery and self-acceptance.

Coach Her on Sex and Sexuality: It is important to talk with your daughter about sex and sexuality in ways appropriate to her age. As she gets older, it becomes increasingly important to help your daughter understand the difference between sexualized images in the media and healthy sexuality. Through a give-and-take discussion, you can help her begin to understand the difference between the media's presentation of sex and sexiness.

You can talk about how sex is frequently portrayed without love, intimacy or emotion, or as part of caring relationships. Help her to cultivate healthy values and beliefs regarding her sexuality. These may include healthy boundaries – how far does she allow herself to go in regard to sex before she is married? If she does have sex with romantic partners how does that impact on her emotionally and relationally? When your daughter is old enough, you can begin to discuss what a mature, healthy, loving relationship in which sex is a part is all about.

Help Her Deal with Life's Struggles: We have to acknowledge that at times, girls experience pain and this is part of life. They need to feel heard and accepted and empathized with. As a parent, you need to stay calm and listen to what she is experiencing without projecting your own experiences onto hers. Your daughter is having a different experience than you did, even if there are surface similarities. She may easily get into depression if you are not close enough to pick her emotional struggles so that you can help her process them. *Be a Playmate:* Having a powerful girl is exciting and energizing. Find activities you both enjoy and do them regularly together. Maybe you both like cooking or having breakfast together or reading books. Try to keep this connection as she gets older. If times ever get tough, you will appreciate this special bond you share. Enjoying a relationship with a daughter creates an environment of freeness where she can share her struggles, embarrassments, hurts and challenges.

Difference between Fantasy and Reality in the Media: Help her avoid the narrow focus on appearance and consumerism that often dominates the media. Like for example, what constitutes beauty in a girl? Is it leanness so that if she is a plump girl she is not good enough? Is it having dreadlocks that makes a young woman cool? While all this may be trendy, help her develop values, likes and beliefs around all aspects of her life. Help her notice the bigger picture, for example, how looking like her latest teen idol can be fun but also connect her with a lot of other stuff she might not have noticed or thought about.

from god with love
Children are a blessing sent from God above for us to care and nurture and most of all to love.
God calls us to be parents and urges us to train our children diligently and when we feel like giving up, our strength He renews.

*Children are a gift from God that He so freely lends to make it through the
childhood years, on Him we must depend.*
*He must have a presence; you see, it must take three the parents, child and
Christ at the center of your parenting.*
*From childhood days to a child full grown his/her joys and hurts are a
parent's own secret. Times of joy and laughter and those times of tears the
times spent raising a child are surely the best of years.*
*There comes that time in life when a child will leave the nest we must send
them off with love and a prayer and leave the rest to God.*

*We've have shared the Word of God, we've taught him/her right from wrong
NOW it's time to let him/her go to write own narrative.*

*The faith instilled, the examples lived, and the lessons taught all gifts that
we've given our children, which will never be forgotten.*

*There are many paths a child can take, right or wrong it maybe but rest
assured that whatever you instilled will sprout and flourish eventually.*

Anonymous author
rEfErENCES

Amato, P. R. (2005). The impact of family formation change on the
cognitive, social, and emotional well-being of the next generation. *The
Future of Children, 15(2)*, 75-96.

Baumrind, D. (1966). Effects of authoritative parental control on child
behavior. *Child Development, 37(4)*, 887-907.
Claire A., Simon D. & Rosalind, E. (Eds.) (2010). *Teenage parenthood:
What's the problem?* London: The Tufnell Press

Conley,T.D.,Ziegler,A.,Moors,A.C.,Matsick,J.L.,& Valentine,B.(2012). A
critical examination of popular assumptions about the benefits and outcomes
of monogamous relationships. *Personality and Social Psychology Review.*

Dancy, R. B. (2012).You are your child's first teacher: Encouraging your
child's natural development from birth to age six (3rd ed.), US: Ten Speed
Press.

Dietz,W.H., Strasburger,V.C. (1991). Children, adolescents and television. *Current Problems Pediatricians*, 21:8–31
Elkind, David (1967). Egocentrism in adolescence. Child Development 38 (4): 1025–1034.
Erikson, E. (1950). *Childhood and society* (1st ed.). New York: Norton

Frankenberger, K.D. (2000). Adolescent egocentrism: a comparison among adolescents and adults. Journal of Adolescence 2000 23: 343–354. Harding, J. (2013) *Child development: An illustrated handbook.* Oxon: Hodder Education.

Johnson, J. G., Cohen, P., Smailes, E. M., Kasen, S., Brook, J. S. (2002). Television viewing and aggressive behavior during adolescence and adulthood. *Science. 295:2468–71.*

Kail, R. V. (2011). Children and their development (6th ed.) (My development lab Series). Englewood Cliffs. N. J. Prentice Hall.
Kenya Violence Against Children Survey (2010)
Laura E. B. (2012). Infants and children: Prenatal through middle childhood. London: Allyn & Bacon.

Maccoby, E. E., & Martin, J. A. (1983). Socialization in the context of the family: Parent–child interaction. In P. H. Mussen & E. M. Hetherington, *Handbook of child psychology: Vol. 4. Socialization, personality, and social development (4th ed.).* New York: Wiley.

McLanahan, S. & Gary, S. (2009). *Growing up with a single parent: What hurts, what helps.* USA. Harvard University Press.

Manning,W. D. & Lamb, K.A. (2003).Adolescent well-being in cohabiting, married, and single-parent families. *Journal of Marriage and the Family,* 65(4), 876-893.

Marilyn, N. A. (Ed.) (1988). *Later language development: Ages nine through nineteen.* Austin, TX: Pro-Ed.

Martin (1998) April Martin, PhD Clinical Psychologist, New York, NY. http://parenthood.library.wisc.edu/Martin/Martin.html 1998

Monaghan,E.,and S.Glickman.(19920.*Hormones and aggressive behavior*. In J. Becker, S. Breedlove, and D. Crews (Eds.), *Behavioral Endocrinology*. Cambridge MA: MIT Press.

Moore, K. A., Jekielek, S. M. & Emig, C. (2002). *Marriage from a child's perspective: How does family structure affect children, and what can we do about it?* Washington, DC. Child Trends.

Payne, V. G., Isaacs, L. D., (2002). *Human motor development: A life span approach*. 5[th]ed. Mountain view, California, Mayfield.
Parke, M. (2003). *Are married parents really better for children? What research says about the effects of family structure on child well-being*
Patterson,C.(1992).Children lesbian and gay parents.*Child Development*, Vol. 63, No. 5, 1025-1042.

Resnick et al., (1997). Protecting adolescents from harm: Findings from the national longitudinal study on adolescent health. *Journal of the American Medical Association* 278, No. 10 823–832.

Ruskin, K. (2014). Retrieved from http://www.drkarenruskin.com/ polyamory-not-healthy-for-children/

Schilmoeller, G. L., Baranowski, M. D., & Higgins, B. S. (1991). Long-term support and personal adjustment of adolescent and older mothers. *Adolescence*, 26, 787 – 797

Sharman, C. Cross, W. and Vennis, D. (2004) *Observing children: A practical guide*. London: Continuum.
Svare, B. (Ed.). 1983. *Hormones and aggressive behavior*. New York. Plenum Press.
Verrier, N. N. (1993). *The primal wound: Understanding the adopted child*. Baltimore, MD: Gateway Press, Inc
https://www.empoweringparents.com/article/rules-boundaries-andolder-children-part-i/

https://www.psychologytoday.com/blog/surviving-your-childsadolescence/201204/parenting-adolescents-and-the-problemsletting-go

https://www.psychologytoday.com/blog/surviving-your-
childsadolescence/201304/attachment-and-detachment-parentingadolescents

http://www.cdc.gov/ncbddd/childdevelopment/positiveparenting/
adolescence2.html
http://community.babycenter.com/post/a27663771/poems_on_
being_a_parent
http://www.babycenter.ca/a1028227/ten-tips-for-raising-a-confidentgirl
http://www.pbs.org/parents/parenting/raising-girls/body-
imageidentity/raising-a-powerful-girl/

http://www.jubilee-centre.org/gender-co-operation-someimplications-of-
gods-design-for-society-by-michael-and-aurielschluter/

https://www.healthychildren.org/English/ages-stages/gradeschool/
Pages/Gender-Identity-and-Gender-Confusion-In-Children.aspx

http://raisingaboy.net/2010/07/raising-a-boy-advice-single-mother/
http://www.babycenter.com/0_10-tips-for-raising-a-well-
roundedboy_10310246.bc

http://www.bounty.com/preschool-2-to-4-years/development/
milestones/bringing-up-boys
http://www.mentoringboys.com/parenting.html Endorsements
aPPrECiaTiON

As little children, we appreciated the way our parents cared for us and
thought they were unparalleled. However, as we grew up, there are times we
found ourselves assailed by the odd mixture of love and hate as we responded
to their requirements. Those were,example, the times when they put
restrictions on our movement and sought to closely monitor our activities.
We wanted independence,yet they were cautious. What we hated most were
the times when they sat us down to evaluate what was happening to us; we
felt unduly judged and as if we were inadequate to manage ourselves.
However, looking back, their effective parenting has made us who we are,
and that is why we recommend this book, for the benefit of other parents, the
wisdom they applied in raising us to be responsible citizens.
Kenna Gachutha and Keega Gakuua

We started parenting with lots of enthusiasm;after all God had graciously given us children. Parenting Kenna and Keega when they were little was enjoyable and easy. Then came the middle childhood and they had emotional, health, social, academic and discipline issues that we needed to address.The adolescent stage was the most chaotic and many times, we thought we had lost it. Parenting with Catherine has been both a joy and a pain since our parenting styles are different; I am a strict disciplinarian and she is more permissive. Now, I appreciate that different parenting styles have both strengths and weaknesses; hence, regulation is neccesary to meet our budding children's needs. With time, Catherine and I have learnt the art of mutually adjusting our parenting methods to meet our children's emerging needs.
Gilbert Gachutha Gakuua